YORKSHIRE TERRIER AND YORKSHIRE TERRIERS

Yorkshire Terrier Total Guide

YORKSHIRE TERRIERS, YORKSHIRE TERRIER PUPPIES, YORKIE DOGS, YORKSHIRE TERRIER TRAINING, YORKIE GROOMING, HEALTH, & MORE!

Susanne Saben

© DYM Worldwide Publishers

DYM Worldwide Publishers

ISBN: 978-1-911355-70-0

Table of Contents

Introduction 12

Chapter 1 – All About Yorkies: History and Origins................15

Origin of the Yorkshire Terrier Pedigree...............15

History of the Yorkshire Terrier 16

What Were Yorkies Bred For?...............................17

Yorkshire Terriers in History and Popular Culture...19

    Smoky 19

    Pasha 20

    Mr. Famous 20

    Wizard of Oz 21

    Cinnamon 21

Yorkies Today – Beloved Family Companions 21

Chapter 2 – What is a Yorkie Like? Knowing the Yorkshire
Terrier 23

Purebred Yorkie – What are the Official Yorkie
Characteristics, and Breed Standards?...................23

Yorkshire Terrier Size – What is the Ideal
Measurement Range? 25

Yorkshire Terrier Weight – How Much does a
Healthy Yorkie Weigh? 26

Yorkie Puppies – What do They Look Like? 27

Yorkie Temperament and Personality 27

Yorkie Hair – What do You Need to Know
About It?..28

Yorkie Coat – What are the Different Types?.........29

Other Yorkie Colors...29

Parti Yorkies 29

Black Yorkies..30

Chocolate Yorkies...30

Coat Types...30

Chapter 3 – Getting a Yorkie Part A: Buying a Yorkshire Terrier – Yorkshire Terrier Price 32

Adult Yorkshire Terrier for Sale – What is the Price? 32

Yorkshire Terrier Puppies for Sale – How Much is It? 33

Miniature Yorkie For Sale – How Much are They? 34

What Should You Consider When Buying a Yorkie? 35

What Should You Keep in Mind and Watch Out When Purchasing a Yorkie?................................38

Chapter 4 – Getting a Yorkie Part B: Yorkshire Terrier Adoption and Rescue 42

Yorkshire Terrier Rescue – What Happened to These Dogs? 43

Yorkie Puppies for Adoption – What are the Things You Need to Consider? 43

Yorkies For Adoption Near Me – Where to Find One? 44

Yorkies For Adoption – What is the Process of Adopting a Yorkie?..45

How to Take Care of a Rescued Yorkshire Terrier? 46

Yorkie Rescue Near Me – What You can do to Help...48

Chapter 5 – Bringing Your Yorkie Home – What Do You Need to Prepare? 50

How to Prepare Your Home for Your Yorkie 50

How to Set Up a Safe Space for Your Yorkie 51

Hazardous Items to Keep Out of Your Yorkie's Reach..53

Introducing Your Yorkie To Your Family – How Should You do It?..54

Bringing A Rescued Yorkie Home........................ 55

Family Members, Children, and Other Pets – How Can You Help Your Yorkie Adjust? 56

Chapter 6 – Yorkie Pet Supplies – What Does Your Dog Need?...58

Yorkie Grooming Kit – What Should You Have?...58

Yorkie Grooming Tools 59

Yorkie Grooming Comb and Brush...................... 60

Yorkie Trimmer 61

Yorkie Shampoo and Yorkie Soap – What is the Best One to Use for Your Dog? 62

Yorkie Puppy Shampoo - What are Safe Ones for Your Baby Yorkie?.................................... 63

Walking with Your Yorkie – What do You Need?....64

Yorkie Harness....................................... 64

Yorkie Dog Collar 66

Yorkie Dog Leash 66

Making Your Yorkie Comfortable – What Does Your Dog Need? 68

Yorkie Dog Beds...................................... 68

Yorkie Dog Carrier 69

Yorkie Dog Crate 70

Yorkie Dog House 71

Yorkie Dog Bowls – What You Need to Make Mealtime Easy and Mess-free for Your Yorkie.......71

Yorkie Dog Toys – What are the Different Types? 72

Yorkie Puppy Chew Toys.............................. 72

Yorkie Exercise and Enrichment Toys................. 73

Yorkie Accessories...74
 Yorkie Dog Clothes................................ 74
 Yorkie Hair Products............................. 76
Yorkie Dog Gate – Does Your Dog Need One? 76
Yorkshire Terrier Snacks – What Can You
Give Your Dog? 77
Chapter 7 – How to Take Care of a Yorkie – Yorkie Care 101 79
Grooming Your Yorkie 79
 Yorkie Hair Care 80
 Different Types of Yorkie Haircuts 82
 Maintaining Your Yorkie's Nails 84
 How to Keep Ticks and Fleas Away 85
Yorkie Puppy Care – What You Need to Know......86
Senior Yorkies – How to Take Care of Your
Yorkshire Terrier in its Old Age 88
Yorkie Exercise – How Much of it does Your
Dog Need? 90
How to Be a Yorkshire Terrier Savvy Owner..........92
Chapter 8 – House Training Your Yorkie – What Skills does
it Need to Know?...93
What You Need to Know Before Housetraining
Your Yorkie 93
How Can You and Your Yorkie Prepare for
Housetraining?..95
Indoor or Outdoor – How Can You Train Your
Yorkie To Do Its Business? 95
Essential Skills and Strategies for Yorkie
Housetraining 96
Do's and Don'ts When Housetraining Your
Yorkie 97
Chapter 9 – Yorkshire Terrier Health and Nutrition 99
Yorkshire Terrier Life Span...............................99

Prolonging Your Yorkie's Life 99

Yorkshire Terrier Health Concerns 101

Yorkshire Terrier Food 102

Eukanuba Yorkshire Terrier 103

Yorkshire Terrier Puppy Food – What is the Best Type? 105

Yorkie Veterinary Care – What does This Breed Need? 106

Yorkie Vitamins – What does Your Dog Need? ...106

Vaccinations – What does Your Yorkie Need? 107

How Can You Keep Your Yorkie Healthy? 108

Chapter 10 – Training Yorkies – Obedience Training...............110

Yorkie Items for Training – What You Need to Have Before Starting Training 111

Yorkie Behavioral Problems – What are the Things You Need to Address? 112

Training A Yorkie Puppy 115

Important Commands Your Yorkie Needs to Master 116

Yorkshire Terrier Training – What are the Best Strategies?..118

Chapter 11 – Yorkshire Terrier Breeding...........................120

What are Your Responsibilities as a Yorkshire Terrier Breeder? 120

Yorkshire Terrier Full Grown – When Can They Start to Breed?....................................122

Yorkie Male – How to Take Care of One for Breeding 122

Female Yorkie – How to Prepare Her for Breeding 123

Baby Yorkies – How to Take Care of New-Born Yorkie Puppies...123

Yorkshire Terrier Breeders – How to Find
Reputable Ones? 126

Chapter 12 – Different Yorkie Mix Breeds.............................. 128

Yorkie Shih Tzu 129

Yorkie Bichon 129

Maltese Yorkie... 130

Yorkie Chihuahua 131

Yorkie Poodle (Or Yorkie-Poo) 132

Chapter 13 – Other Yorkie Information You Need to Know 133

Miniature Yorkies and Teacup Yorkies – What
are They and What You Should Know about
Them? 133

Yorkshire Terrier Clubs and Yorkie Lovers
Groups – Why and How to Join One?................. 135

Yorkie Show Dogs – What Do You Need
to Know?... 136

Other Dog Competitions Where You Can Enter
Your Yorkshire Terrier....................................... 137

How to Build A Stronger Bond with Your
Yorkshire Terrier 138

Conclusion 140

Bonus Chapter: Yorkshire Terrier Rescue Shelters in the USA 142

Introduction

The Yorkshire Terrier, lovingly nicknamed the "Yorkie," is one of the top favorite and popular dog breeds. In fact, the breed ranks ninth in the American Kennel Club's Most Popular Dog list. The Yorkie is classified under the Toy Group. However, do not underestimate its adorable face and tiny structure. This small dog packs a big and feisty personality and is even known as a "tomboy toy" dog. It is known to be brave, determined, and energetic. It will not hesitate to face a bigger dog and may sometimes forget how small it is compared to its adversary!

Based on the American Kennel Club's (AKC) picture of the ideal Yorkie, it sports a long flowing coat that is bluish and tan on parts of the face, and from the skull's base to the end of the tail. Its hair also hangs straight and even on both sides of its body. Its figure is neat, compact and well-proportioned. It carries its head high, giving the impression of confidence, vigor, and self-confidence.

Before it rested on the laps of socialites and Hollywood stars, the Yorkshire Terrier started from humble beginnings. The breed belonged to the working class during England's Industrial Revolution and was used to hunt rats in mills in Yorkshire, in Northern England. It still has retained its hunting instincts, which is why it may sometimes display aggressive behavior, at times.

The Yorkshire Terrier is a healthy and robust dog.

Perhaps the biggest challenge to owning a Yorkie is in the grooming department. If you are keen on maintaining a Yorkshire Terrier for show competitions, be prepared to invest a lot of time, energy, and money in keeping its long coat pristine!

The Yorkshire Terrier is a healthy and robust dog. However, it can still contract certain health conditions ranging from negligible to fatal, if not attended to. You may be surprised to hear a Yorkie snort or wheeze. This is known as Pharyngeal Gag Reflex, or reverse sneezing, and is caused by spasms coming from the larynx. These should not be something to worry about and subsides when the dog is able to calm down and breathe normally. Other serious medical illnesses you should watch out for are hypoglycemia, Legg-Perthes Disease, and Retinal Dysplasia.

Is the Yorkshire Terrier the right dog for you? This breed will make a great companion if you prefer a small dog that is easy to carry around. It will do well in any living space and can easily adjust to apartment living. This dog is also perfect if you want one that has lesser food requirements and has a longer lifespan. Yorkies are also affectionate, and love to cuddle with their owners!

The Yorkie might not be for you if you're looking for one that can double as a guard dog. People would assume that Yorkies make great companions for children, but this dog can get aggressive and may bite your kids when play turns to rough-housing.

This book is your complete guide to the essential information you need to have in owning and caring for a Yorkie. The chapters of this book will cover topics that include important Yorkie supplies, health and nutrition, and Yorkie breeding. You're about to explore the wonderful world of the Yorkshire Terrier, and you'll soon be well on your way to being and to knowing this loving and loyal companion well!

CHAPTER 1

All About Yorkies: History and Origins

One might think that the Yorkshire Terrier is all about glitz and glamor. However, you'll be surprised to know that it was a favored companion of the middle class during England's Industrial Revolution. This chapter discusses the Yorkie's evolution throughout the years, and how it became the dog that everyone loves today.

Origin of the Yorkshire Terrier Pedigree

Before this black and tan beauty existed, several breeds were combined to produce what we know as the Yorkshire Terrier today. The breed's ancestors can be traced to the Waterside Terrier, Paisley Terrier, and the Clydesdale Terrier. These dog breeds originated from Scotland and were brought to England in the middle of the nineteenth century. The Waterside Terrier is a tiny Scottish dog with a long blue-grey coat. The now-extinct Paisley and Clydesdale Terriers had flowy, silvery coats, and erect ears.

Huddersfield Ben

Perhaps the most important dog in the Yorkshire Terrier history is Huddersfield Ben. He is considered as the foundation sire of the Yorkie breed, and known as the "father of modern Yorkies." He was a champion show dog, having won over 70 awards and recognitions, in his lifetime. He became the most in-demand stud dog of the time, and although he was bigger than today's standard Yorkie (11 lb.), he consistently produced litters of lesser weight and smaller size.

Huddersfield Ben was born in the town where he received his name, in Yorkshire, England. He was born in 1865, but sadly lived for only six years when he met an unfortunate accident of being crushed by a passing carriage. Huddersfield Ben is affectionately remembered as the "best stud dog of his breed during his lifetime, and one of the most remarkable dogs of any breed that ever lived."

History of the Yorkshire Terrier

The Yorkshire Terrier's history is relatively new, as the breed is not very old, compared to many of today's breeds. In the middle of the 18th century, England's Industrial Revolution was in full swing, and many miners and mill workers from Scotland came to England for work and brought along with them their tiny Terrier dogs.

The breed originated in the county of its namesake (Yorkshire) in northern England, and first appeared in a bench show. During this breed's early stages, it was called the Broken-haired Scotch Terrier. It carried this name for nine years, until one day a reporter commented that its name should be changed to "Yorkshire Terrier," due to the improvement of its appearance since it first arrived in the area. In 1874, the name Yorkshire Terrier was officially recognized.

During the later Victorian Period, the Yorkshire Terrier became prominent among royalty, nobility, and upper-class society. It was at this time that the breed was uplifted from its lowly role of rat hunter to companions of the rich and royalty.

The Yorkie eventually made its way to the United States in 1872 and was officially recognized by the American Kennel Club in 1885.

What Were Yorkies Bred For?

Upon seeing a Yorkie, one would assume the dog has always lived a life of luxury. You would be surprised to know that these dogs were bred to kill rats and other vermin that hid in tiny spaces. Millers and miners would take their Yorkies into their work and living spaces, to kill the pests that resided there.

Upon seeing a Yorkie, one would assume the dog has always lived a life of luxury. You would be surprised to know that these dogs were bred to kill rats and other vermin, that hid in tiny spaces in mills and mines.

Yorkies also showed remarkable skill and success in hunting wild animals that lived in dens and burrows hiding on the forest floor. Hunters would take their Yorkies to track foxes, badgers, and other small to medium game. When these animals faced threats and were trapped in their dens, they displayed aggressive behavior to protect themselves and their offspring. The Yorkie remained unfazed despite the wild animals' hostile stance and would pursue them without hesitation.

Yorkshire Terriers in History and Popular Culture

Smoky

A famous Yorkie called Smoky brought great honor to her breed and skyrocketed its popularity by becoming a World War II heroine. She was initially discovered in a foxhole by an American soldier and was later bought by Cpl. Bill Wynne. She became a part of the 5th Air Force in the Pacific and was even present in 150 air raids and 12 sea missions!

Smoky had an important role in communications when Wynne used her to help string phone lines between outposts during their deployment in the Philippines. Her small physique and intelligence made the mission possible. She was able to maneuver herself inside a culvert that was 8 in. (20.32 cm.) in diameter and 70 ft. (21.33 m.) long. If it were not for Smoky, it would have taken a team of men and several days, to do the job.

She also did some death-defying stunts, when she was packed with a custom-made parachute and jumped out from a 30-foot tower (9.14 m.). This feat earned her the first prize mascot, in the Yank Contest.

Smoky also became the first therapy dog, when she accompanied nurses in their rounds, treating wounded soldiers. After the war ended, Wynn and Smoky traveled around the United States, particularly in Hollywood where the dog performed on local television programs, to the delight of many.

Wynne later wrote a memoir about Smoky entitled *Yorkie Doodle Dandy*, chronicling her wartime efforts and extraordinary life. She died in 1957, and several memorials were built in her honor.

Pasha

Tricia Nixon, daughter of former US President Richard Nixon, owned a Yorkie they named Pasha. The little Yorkie spent much time with Tricia, but would occasionally be spotted with Richard Nixon's wife, Thelma Catherine "Pat" Nixon. Pasha was also present during the 30th anniversary of the March of Dimes. Shortly after that, Nixon declared his candidacy for the presidential race.

Julie Nixon Eisenhower, Tricia's younger sister, wrote a children's story about Pasha. Entitled "Pasha Passes By," it painted an amusing story about the dog escaping from his kennel and exploring the White House.

Mr. Famous

Audrey Hepburn, Hollywood's Golden Age superstar, owned a Yorkshire Terrier she named Mr. Famous. Hepburn's loving ownership of Mr. Famous introduced the Yorkie to the glamorous life of celebrities and started the trend of having an adorable lap dog, as a companion.

Mr. Famous starred alongside Hepburn in her movies, among them *Funny Face* (1957), and appeared with her in numerous magazine covers.

Mr. Famous was unfortunately killed in an accident during the production of Hepburn's movie, *The Children's Hour* (1961). Hepburn grieved the loss of her beloved friend. Her husband at that time, Mel Ferrer, gave Hepburn a new Yorkie whom they named Assam of Assam.

Wizard of Oz

In the classic children's story, *The Wonderful Wizard of Oz* (1900), written by L. Frank Baum and illustrated by W.W. Denslow, Toto the dog was originally thought to be a Yorkshire Terrier.

The book does not explicitly state Toto's breed, but readers concluded such as Toto was described as a "little black dog with long silky hair."

In the film version of the book, a female Cairn Terrier played the role of Toto.

Cinnamon

The hit comedy series, *The Big Bang Theory*, also features a Yorkshire Terrier that is owned by the show's character, Rajesh Koothrappali. In the twentieth episode of its fifth season, characters Howard and Bernadette Wolowitz give Rajesh a Yorkie, to console him after his date ended unfavorably. The latter names the dog Cinnamon, and spoils her excessively.

Yorkies Today – Beloved Family Companions

The days of chasing rats in mills and factories are long behind for the Yorkies, and they now enjoy a much more pampered and comfortable life. They are continuously ranked among the most popular dog breeds in many countries and regions, among them the US, UK, Australia, and much of Europe. They have become beloved family companions, to which they reciprocate with affection and loyalty.

The modern-day Yorkie is a tad smaller than the ones from Huddersfield Ben's days. They are also seen more as a fashion accessory than a hunter from decades past. The Yorkie may have been provided with a comfortable abode by its doting owners, but it still requires and enjoys an active routine.

CHAPTER 2

What is a Yorkie Like?
Knowing the Yorkshire Terrier

This chapter defines the official standard appearance of the Yorkshire Terrier, as described by the American Kennel Club. It will give you the information on how a Yorkshire Terrier must ideally look, and what other qualities it must exhibit, to be considered as healthy and conforming to the Breed's standards.

Purebred Yorkie – What are the Official Yorkie Characteristics, and Breed Standards?

There are two sides to the Yorkie's appearance. If you plan to own one for show competitions, your Yorkie must strictly adhere to the American Kennel Club's conformation standards for the Yorkshire Terrier. On the other hand, if you do not intend to let your Yorkie join dog shows, you can opt for a lower maintenance look.

The AKC describes the standard Yorkshire Terrier as a "long-haired toy terrier whose blue and tan coat is parted on the face, and from the base of the skull to the end of the tail. The coat should hang down evenly, and quite straight down, on each side of the body. The physique is neat, compact, and well-proportioned. The dog's high head carriage and confident manner should give the appearance of vigor and self-importance."

The Yorkie's physique is neat, compact and well-proportioned. The dog's high head carriage and confident manner should give the appearance of vigor and self-importance."

The Yorkie's head is small and flat on top. Its skull is "not too prominent or round." Its muzzle is not too elongated, and its bite is not undershot, nor overshot. A scissor or level bite is an acceptable appearance of the teeth.

The Yorkie's nose is black. The eyes are medium-sized and not too prominent, and the rims are dark. The color of the eyes is dark and sparkling, expressing sharpness and intelligence. Its ears should be small, V-shaped, stand erect, and not set too far apart.

The body is well-proportioned and very compact. The back is short, and the line is leveled. Its height at the shoulders is the same with the rump. The tail is docked to a medium length and is carried slightly higher than the level of the back.

The forelegs should be straight, and the elbows should not protrude nor angle inward. The hind legs should also be straight when viewed from behind, but stifles (hind limb joints) are moderately bent when viewed from the sides. Its feet should be round, and the toenails are black. Dewclaws on the Yorkies' hind legs are typically removed and may also be taken out from the forelegs.

Yorkshire Terrier Size – What is the Ideal Measurement Range?

The ideal height for the Yorkshire Terrier is 8 in. to 9 in. (20.32 to 22.86 cm.) tall at the shoulder.

Yorkie Size Records

The Yorkie has landed a place in world records, particularly in the smallest dog category. In 1945, a 2.5 in. (6.35 cm.) Yorkie from Blackburn, England, was the smallest dog recorded in history. Named Sylvia by her owner, Arthur Maples, she was only that small when measured at the shoulder. From her nose to the tip of her tail she measured 3.5 in. (8.89 cm.), and only weighed 4 oz. (113.39 g.).

The Guinness Book of World Records recognized two Yorkies as the smallest living dogs. From 1995 to 2002, a 4.7 in. (11.93 cm.) Yorkie named Big Boss held the title. The next title holder was

Thumbelina (2005), a Yorkie that was 5.5 in. (13.97 cm.) tall, and 8 in. (20.32 cm.) long.

Yorkshire Terrier Weight – How Much Does a Healthy Yorkie Weigh?

The previous weight standard described by the AKC for the Yorkshire Terrier was 4 lb. (1.81 kg.) However, it is now changed from 4 lb. to a maximum weight of 7 lb. (3.17 kg.), for a fully grown adult Yorkie.

A Yorkie weighing less than the described weight is considered to be too small for the breed standard and may be more susceptible to health conditions. On the other end, some Yorkies exceed the maximum weight. These Yorkies can weigh between 8 to 10 lbs. (3.62 to 4.53 kg.).

Yorkies that are larger than average may attribute their size to bigger bone structure. This can be caused by breeders who have chosen a breeding pair that did not conform to the standard Yorkie characteristics. Another factor that causes Yorkies to be larger than the average is that one pup can just turn out larger than the rest of its littermates. It may have inherited genes from generations back, with the forefathers having bigger body structures.

However, if your Yorkie's weight is more than 9 lb. (4.08 kg.), your veterinarian may need to evaluate your dog and see if it needs a weight loss program (depending on the body mass index).

Yorkie Puppies – What Do They Look Like?

Before a Yorkshire Terrier comes to its long and flowing coat glory, it starts out as a pup covered with short and soft fur, that is black with tan spots. Even if you see a pup that is black all over, you will discover a few tan fluffs, if you look closely. You can also see these spots on the muzzle, under the tail, the outer part of the hind and front legs, and above the eyes. Other areas are on the inner side of the front paws, armpits, chest, and hind paws.

Newborn Yorkie pups weigh approximately 2.5 oz. (.07 kg.). Their eyes will remain closed until the second or third week, after birth.

Yorkies mature quite fast and will typically reach their adult appearance when they are a year old. When the Yorkie pup starts to grow, changes in its coat color typically start on the head. The chest and paws turn lighter, and the silvery/steel color starts to show on the neck, shoulder, back, and waist. You will be able to see the change between the roots and the rest of the coat when you view your Yorkie from above.

Yorkie Temperament and Personality

Yorkies have big personalities despite their tiny size. As per the AKC's standards, the ideal Yorkie temperament exudes confidence, vigor, and self-importance. Most of the time Yorkies forget how small they are, and they would not hesitate to face a larger dog. They are affectionate and fiercely loyal to their owners.

Yorkies can easily adapt to different surroundings and are easy to carry around. They are also sociable and outgoing and would need daily interaction and socialization with other people and dogs.

There are some behaviors you will need to address early on. You will need to assert your position as the leader of the "pack," or else the Yorkie will become your boss. Do not tolerate negative behavior such as incessant yapping, barking, and pulling, lest you will be living with a very noisy, spoiled, and arrogant dog.

Yorkie Hair – What Do You Need to Know about It?

Beyond its aesthetic appeal, there are more interesting things to know about the Yorkie's hair. Its coat is comprised of human-like hair, not fur. Unlike double-coated dogs such as the Husky, German Shepherd, and Labradors where their undercoat continuously grows and sheds, Yorkies are among the breeds who have single coats. Their hair keeps growing until it reaches its maximum length. This also makes it less likely for dander (dead skin cells which cause allergic reactions), to stick. It also does not shed like these other dogs, but you'll still be cleaning up long strands of hair.

You will need to maintain the quality, quantity, and texture of the Yorkie's coat. Ideally, it should appear glossy, fine and silky. If you are planning to have it compete in dog shows, or just simply want to have it sport a longer cut, it must appear straight, and no wavy parts should be seen.

The AKC also designates that the hair is to be trimmed to floor length, to allow the dog to move easily.

There are two ways to keep hair from falling from its face: tied with one bow in the center or parted in the middle and tied with two bows.

The hair on the Yorkie's muzzle can also grow very long and should be trimmed short on the ears' tips.

Yorkie Coat – What are the Different Types?

There are only four-color pairings that the AKC recognizes: black and tan, black and gold, blue and tan, and blue and gold.

These colors should also show in the right areas. The body must be blue or black starting from the neck up to the tip of the tail. The head should show a golden tan or gold hue on the fall. The color should be richer on the ears and muzzle. The tan and gold color should also appear on the chest, and no higher than the elbow on the front legs, and the stifle on the hind legs.

Other Yorkie Colors

Parti Yorkies

Parti is the only alternative Yorkie color that the AKC accepts. They are still purebred Yorkies but have white streaks on their coats.

Parti Yorkies were already around in the 18th century but were considered as unfavorable by breeders and experts. They did not want their Yorkies to be known to produce pups that did not adhere to the standard colors. Because of this, the breeders gave away these pups to people under the condition they would not divulge their source.

Black Yorkies

Producing a full black Yorkie, from purebred parents, is impossible. The only way to get an all-black Yorkie is if it is crossed with another breed that has an entirely solid black coat.

Chocolate Yorkies

Chocolate Yorkies have dark to light brown coats. This appearance can be caused by a double recessive Chocolate gene, that is present in one of the parents, or a cross-breed of a Yorkie and another breed with a brown coat.

Coat Types

Puppy Coat

The puppy Yorkie will have a thicker and softer coat. This provides extra protection to keep it warm until the pup grows into its adult coat. The coat's color is also darker, with more prominent black spots, and tan highlights. This appearance will start to fade as the pup grows and develops over the first 24 months.

Silky Coat

The silky coat is the AKC standard. It must appear long, straight, and glossy with an almost metallic shine. If you choose to have your Yorkie sport a silky coat, it ideally must be maintained in a proper show grooming style. The coat is frequently trimmed and made to appear as if a skirt of hair surrounds its body and evenly touches the floor. The muzzle must be kept neat, and the hair on its head is tied in a bow.

Wire / Cotton Coat

Yorkies who have this type of coat are probably not purebred and are an offspring of a parent who has a wavy or wooly coat. No matter how much you brush it, the coat will not appear silky and long but instead becomes more textured. Wire coats typically do not grow more than a few inches and will have an appearance of a double-coat. This type of coat is also susceptible to matting. Regular brushing and grooming are needed to avoid this.

CHAPTER 3

Getting a Yorkie Part A: Buying a Yorkshire Terrier – Yorkshire Terrier Price

Before buying a Yorkie, you must seriously weigh the pros and cons, and assess if this is indeed the best breed for you. Some things you need to learn about are hereditary health conditions and the dog's temperament. This beautiful breed also demands a hefty price tag, so you should consider if you have the budget for it.

The most important thing you need to keep in mind is to purchase your Yorkie from a reputable breeder. This will ensure you that all necessary precautions and care has been administered from the time of breeding to the dam's pregnancy, and post-natal care.

Adult Yorkshire Terrier for Sale – What is the Price?

A fully-grown, show-standard adult Yorkshire Terrier can cost anywhere from 800 to 10,000 USD. It will still depend on the breeder's investment and care throughout the breeding process and the dog's pregnancy. Yorkies with this price tag are often bred from a champion line and have a high-quality pedigree. The more titles and recognition a Yorkie has earned, the more expensive and highly-valued it will be.

Breeders who own such high-class Yorkies will typically find a mate for their dogs of the same caliber. Some breeders will even travel to another state just to have their Yorkie breed with a high-level sire or dam.

Yorkies that are AKC- registered are priced higher than those who that are not. The registration process requires fees before it is completed. The breeder will account that factor when pricing his or her Yorkie.

Be careful of pet shops and backyard breeders who sell Yorkies at low prices. More often than not, the environment and treatment of the parents and pups are unhealthy and unsanitary. They also do not execute proper health screenings and medications.

Yorkshire Terrier Puppies for Sale – How Much is It?

An AKC-registered breeder would typically price his or her Yorkie pup at around 1,200 to 2,000 USD, and above. These pups usually have complete certification and documents concerning their health and pedigree.

An AKC-registered breeder would typically price his or her Yorkie pup at around 1,200 to 2,000 USD, and above.

Another option you can consider when acquiring a Yorkie pup is to buy one without papers and registration. You can expect to pay for a Yorkie with this status around 600 to 1,200 USD. Again, be wary of sellers who price Yorkies cheaply. Don't ever think that you got one for a bargain, most of the time these dogs have poor health conditions, and you will be paying more for veterinary bills.

Miniature Yorkie for Sale – How Much are They?

Miniature and Teacup Yorkshire Terriers have somehow acquired a novelty status. People are amused to see a Yorkie that is smaller than the standard size. However, these dogs are severely undersized and are more vulnerable to health concerns. If you insist on a teacup or miniature Yorkie, expect to pay around 2,500 to 5,000 USD.

Yorkies that weigh less than 4 lbs. (1.81 kg.) have a higher probability that they are severely inbred, and so can lead to an abnormal immune system, physical mutations, and behavioral problems.

What Should You Consider When Buying a Yorkie?

Your WHY

Before buying a Yorkie, you first need to know WHY you want one, and what lifestyle you want your Yorkie to have.

Perhaps you want to have a Yorkie as your companion and not have to worry about the pressures of show competitions. You are also not keen on breeding the dog as a means of making a profit. If this is the case, you can find a reputable breeder who prices his or her puppies in the middle range. You will probably encounter a breeder who does not have documents or registration for his or her puppies, and maybe you don't mind as long as you can own a Yorkie. You need to remember that this is a risk that you must be willing to take.

Maybe you want to own a Yorkie that you want to participate in show exhibitions. Be prepared to invest a large amount of money in purchasing the Yorkie and maintaining it. Visit dog shows to connect with other Yorkie breeders and owners. This way you can find the best breeder, from which to make a purchase.

Health Conditions

An important process of evaluating a Yorkie pup you may want to own, is investigating its health history. You need to know the pup's parents, and if there have been any medical conditions that its ancestors had. The best way you can do this is visiting the breeder's kennel. By assessing the kennel's overall environment and looking at the dogs living there, you will know a lot more about the pup. Visiting the kennel will also let you see how the breeder takes care of his or her dogs.

Responsible breeders spend a lot of time, effort and energy to meet the American Kennel Club or the Canadian Kennel Club's standards of the breed's health. Through breeding, they also aim to reduce the risk of hereditary health concerns.

Here are some medical conditions you need to ask your breeder about:

- **Patellar Luxation.** Also known as "floating kneecaps." This happens when the kneecap or patella slips and becomes dislocated. It will come back to its normal position when the quadricep muscles in the hind legs relax and lengthen. You may see dogs show abnormal hindlimb movements, skipping, or lameness. This can be caused by genetic malformation or trauma and can start to exhibit four months after the pup is born.

- **Tracheal Collapse.** This happens when the trachea's cartilage is not correctly formed at birth or degenerates due to old age. Symptoms of this condition include dry coughing, difficulty during exercise, respiratory distress, and gagging while eating or drinking.

- **Portosystemic Shunts (PSS).** Also known as liver shunts and can even occur as early as the pup is still in the mother's womb. This is due to an abnormal development that causes the blood from the intestine to only pass partly through the liver. The remaining blood mixes into the general circulation. The liver will not be able to fully filter out toxins, which causes your dog to become ill. Your Yorkie will episodically exhibit the symptoms of this disease and is more noticeable after meal times. Some of the things your dog will experience include ataxia, seizures, blindness, and head pressing.

- **Intervertebral Disc Disease (or ruptured discs).** Caused by the degeneration of one or more intervertebral disks. It is a neurological disorder that can inflict mild to severe pain and can cause partial to complete paralysis.

Yorkshire Terrier needs and behavior

You will need to accept and prepare for the Yorkie's needs and behavior. If the following are things you are not ready to handle, then perhaps the Yorkie is not the best breed for you.

- **Barking.** Yorkies like to bark a lot. They are known for constantly yapping, although this can be addressed with proper training. If you find this annoying and prefer a quieter dog, then it is best to look for another breed to own.

- **Housebreaking difficulties.** Surprisingly, the Yorkie is one of the breeds that is challenging to house train. You will need to be patient in teaching your Yorkie how to do its business properly, or else you will be picking up after it its whole life. It will need much time to master this skill. If you do not have the time to spare for training, then perhaps the Yorkie is not for you.

- **Grooming.** If you want to enjoy the Yorkie's gorgeous long coat, you will need to brush it daily. You can still choose to have it sport a puppy cut by keeping it short. Whatever you choose, you will need to commit to a regular grooming routine to keep your Yorkie healthy and neat.

- **Separation anxiety.** If you are not present in your home for long periods of time, it is best not to choose a Yorkie for a pet. It is prone to suffering from separation anxiety if it is left alone for too long. It can channel this distress through excessive barking, destructive chewing, and depression.

What Should You Keep in Mind and Watch Out When Purchasing a Yorkie?

You have ticked your checklist about why you want a Yorkie, and now you are ready to get one. Do extensive research where you can buy a Yorkie from a reputable breeder and avoid pet shops and backyard breeders at all costs. Dogs from pet shops are often produced from puppy mills, where breeding pairs are living in unsafe conditions. This often produces pups who have an array of health concerns.

Here are some things to look out for during the buying process from a breeder:

Documents and registration

This informs you of the dog's pedigree and is usually issued by the American Kennel Club/Canadian Kennel Club. It holds details about the dog's family tree. It will also show you descriptions and ratings, and the dog's health history. These documents are an assurance that you are dealing with an honest and responsible breeder.

Questions to ask the breeder

When you have found a responsible and reputable breeder, here are some things you can inquire to help you evaluate the pup he or she is selling, and what kind of care he or she has given unto the pup:

1. Does the breeder guarantee a full refund of the purchase price in writing on the bill of sale if the dog contracts medical conditions such as liver shunts, Legg-Calve-Perthes disease, or congestive heart failure within the first five years of its life?

2. How old the puppy is, what kind and how many vaccines it has received. Also, ask if the puppy is already dewormed.

3. Ask if the breeder will issue a guarantee in writing on the bill of sale and immediately transfer the blue slip, or will the breeder hold it until the neutering/spaying is done?

4. What kind of food and how much has the pup been eating?

5. Are the pups already examined by a veterinarian? What is the veterinarian's name, clinic and contact details? It would be ideal to visit the pup's veterinarian the day you pick it up from the breeder.

6. Ask the breeder if you can see the breeding pair, especially the dam. If you can, try to feel the dog's body, in most cases you will be able to tell if it has a sturdy structure, or if it is too thin and frail.

7. Request to see the breeder's kennel. You will need to assess the dog's environment and see if it has been growing in a clean, healthy and safe place.

8. See if you can ask for contacts of the breeder's previous buyers. If you can locate one, ask for a review or feedback of his or her after-purchase care, and how the dog is doing after the buyer was able to get it from the breeder.

Red Flags

Always seek to visit the breeder's kennel and be very cautious of ones who suggest a meet-up place to conduct the transaction. There is a high probability that the breeder is hiding unfavorable conditions that might dissuade you from buying.

Never buy a Yorkie online where you can make a purchase using your credit card and the breeder will send the dog to your home. Buying in this manner will never let you find out about the dam and her litter's living conditions, and you will not see the pup personally. You will not be able to ask the breeder those important questions immediately, and so putting yourself and the dog at risk.

Be wary of breeders who sell pups that are too young, especially if they are under 12 weeks old. The pup needs this time to get nourishment from its mother, as well as learn instinctive and natural skills from her and its littermates.

If you see a breeder selling two or more breeds other than the Yorkie, he or she could be operating a puppy mill. A reputable breeder focuses only on breeding Yorkshire Terriers.

Never purchase a Yorkie from breeders who advertise "special" ones, like teacups, or rare colors like blue, steel, chocolate or golden. They could claim that these dogs are "unique" and demand a heftier price. There is a high probability this is a scam.

CHAPTER 4

Getting a Yorkie Part B: Yorkshire Terrier Adoption and Rescue

I f you love Yorkies and wish you could do more for the breed, you might want to consider adopting one from a rescue shelter instead of buying from a breeder. By choosing this option, you give a Yorkie another chance at life and provide a loving home for it.

About 3 million dogs end up in shelters every year, and most of the fates of these dogs are unfortunate. There are only so many dogs that shelters can care for. If the dogs do not get adopted, many must be euthanized them to keep the population under control.

This chapter will discuss what you need to know when adopting a Yorkshire Terrier, and what other things you can do to help out.

Yorkshire Terrier Rescue – What Happened to These Dogs?

There are many reasons why a Yorkie ends up in a rescue shelter. One is due to a person's hasty decision to buy a Yorkie because he or she was enamored upon laying eyes on the adorable pup. No due diligence was taken before the purchase, and the new owner finds out he or she cannot keep up with the demands of caring for a Yorkie.

Yorkshire Terriers are wonderful dogs and have become immensely popular. However, not all people are suited to own a Yorkie, and unfortunately, some Yorkies end up with these kinds of people.

Another reason is a drastic change has come to the family that leaves them no choice, but to surrender it to a shelter. These situations could range from financial burdens, being physically unable to care for the dog anymore, divorce, and relocating to another area that does not allow pets. A Yorkie can even run away or escape and get picked up by a rescue shelter. Sometimes a stroke of bad luck falls on these dogs, and it is not their fault. The fact is that most of the dogs in these scenarios are healthy and are just waiting for a loving family to adopt them.

Yorkie Puppies for Adoption – What are the Things You Need to Consider?

Most Yorkies that end up in the shelter are adults. Before adopting a Yorkie, here are some factors you need to consider seeing if having one suits your family's needs and lifestyle:

- **Young children.** Adopting an adult Yorkie in a family with young children may not be a good idea. Rescued Yorkies may have experienced physical and emotional trauma. Kids tend to roughhouse with dogs and may cause further stress to a recovering rescued Yorkie. A Yorkie will also not hesitate to bite when it is distressed, and your children can get injured when this happens.

- **Valuable possessions.** If you have a lot of valuable and expensive possessions lying around your home, it would be better to adopt an adult Yorkie that is past the teething stage.

- **You are out of the house for long periods of time.** As explained in the previous chapter, Yorkies can suffer from separation anxiety.

- **Potty breaks.** This is another reason to consider adopting an adult rescue Yorkie. Pups will frequently need to go to potty since their bladders cannot hold much when they are younger. Puppies can only hold their bladder for one hour for each month from birth (for example, a two-month-old puppy will need to take a potty break every two hours; a three-year-old puppy will need to go every three hours). If you are out for work during the day, a puppy may not be the best pet for you at the time. Adult Yorkies will not leave as much mess as a puppy does.

Yorkies for Adoption Near Me – Where to Find One?

If you have determined for yourself that you are ready to adopt a Yorkshire Terrier, the first step you can take is contacting your local chapter of Society for the Prevention of Cruelty to Animals (SPCA) and identifying animal shelters in your area.

There are some Yorkshire Terrier rescue shelters that can be found in the United States, Canada, and the United Kingdom. Some rescue shelters focus on the geographical location, while others concentrate on rescuing a specific breed. The resource list that is included in this book will provide you a list of locations to help you get started in finding rescued Yorkshire Terriers. Once you have identified a shelter where you can adopt a Yorkie, be sure to personally visit it so you can see how the dogs are thriving, how they are cared for by the staff, and ask the questions that you need to know about the dog.

Yorkies For Adoption – What Is the Process of Adopting a Yorkie?

Once you have located a rescue shelter to adopt a Yorkie, it is time to undergo the adoption process.

1. Fill out the rescue shelter's application form. Once received, it will be under review by the rescue staff.

2. If the staff finds your qualifications favorable, they will conduct a phone interview with you. They will inquire about you, your family, your lifestyle, and how a Yorkie will fit into the picture.

3. The rescue staff will contact your veterinarian (if applicable) for a reference check. This will allow them to assess how often you sought your veterinarian for check-ups, and other actions your past (or present) pet had with your veterinarian.

4. If you passed steps 2 and 3, a rescue staff or volunteer would conduct a home visit to see if your house is an ideal place for a Yorkie to live.

5. Once you have passed all of the criteria of being an eligible owner of a rescued Yorkie, the staff will contact and inform you that you can now take home one of their dogs.

You can also request to be on a waiting list for a Yorkshire Terrier if there is none available for adoption at the moment. The whole process can take about a week to a few months.

How to Take Care of a Rescued Yorkshire Terrier?

Caring for a rescued Yorkie is essentially similar to getting one from a reputable breeder. You will need to get basic supplies like food, leash, and harness or collar. Ideally, you should have this on hand before your Yorkie arrives home.

However, there are some items where you need to step up a notch. Be careful with the type of food you will get for your Yorkie. Most rescued dogs suffer from malnutrition and inadequate nourishment. Check with your veterinarian for the best type of dog food that will restore your Yorkie to its optimum health.

Having a playpen or a fenced area will provide your rescue Yorkie a safe space. Shyness or fear are typical behaviors exhibited by Yorkies and having this area can give it a sense of comfort and protection. It will also need an area for housetraining, and the playpen can provide this space. You may opt to place pee-pads in the corner of the pen.

Having its own area can give it a sense of comfort and protection.

You may also want to provide your Yorkie, a canine orthopedic bed. There's a high chance that it has been sleeping on hard surfaces during its time in the shelter. This may have affected its elbows, hips, and back.

Another important item to have is a Yorkie grooming kit. Yorkies from rescue shelters often have unhealthy skin and hair. This may be due to long periods of not having a proper grooming routine. Shelters also need to budget their expenses, and often times choose lower quality grooming products. Before bathing your Yorkie, be sure to have it checked by your veterinarian to see if it has any skin conditions that need to be treated.

A recommended shampoo mixture is oatmeal and aloe vera, and following it with a moisturizing conditioner to restore its coat to health. If you find any soreness, redness, irritated areas, or parts with thinning hair, you may want to apply skin rescue lotion on these areas. If the paws are dry, peeling or cracked, you can apply paw wax to help them heal. A dry nose can be treated with nose butter to make it moisturized.

Yorkies can suffer from severe dental conditions, and this is usually the case for dogs in shelters. Without administering regular dental care, the Yorkie is more susceptible to developing tooth decay. This can lead to the teeth falling out or rotting and can lead to infections. Part of the first things you need to do when getting a rescued Yorkie is to bring it to the veterinarian and let it have an overall examination, including dental health. The veterinarian specializing in dog's oral health can either conduct a root canal or extraction on any teeth that are already decaying.

Once the dog is cleared of any dental problems, establish a daily dental routine. Use a quality dog toothpaste that is plaque-fighting and non-foaming. Use a small toothbrush that fits your Yorkie or a finger-brush that can be easily inserted in your Yorkie's mouth. You can also add water supplements to its dog bowl that can kill bacteria. Buy chew toys that also work in helping keep its teeth healthy.

Yorkie Rescue Near Me – What You Can do to Help

The good news for abandoned Yorkies is that there are no-kill shelters which house dogs indefinitely and allow volunteers to foster them. You can become a foster parent, and by doing this, you can help both the dog and the shelter that cares for it.

Fostering allows the shelter to fully know the Yorkie's personality based on the foster parent's experience with it. This will give future adoptive owners an in-depth view of the dog's temperament.

Part of your responsibility in becoming a foster parent is to open your home to the rescue Yorkie and provide it with the care it needs. The rescue Yorkie can stay with you for a few days, weeks, or even months.

However, when it is time for the Yorkie to come home to its new family, you will need to be prepared to say goodbye.

Fostering is also a way for you to test the waters and see if the Yorkie is indeed the breed for you. Your reward for becoming a foster parent is being on the priority list when a Yorkie becomes available for adoption.

CHAPTER 5

Bringing Your Yorkie Home – What do You Need to Prepare?

J ust like welcoming a newborn babe into your home, you want to be as prepared as possible when your Yorkie arrives. You don't want to have to improvise ad-hoc solutions to your Yorkie's needs. It is vital to anticipate what the scenarios are, get the necessary equipment, and establish parameters to keep your Yorkie safe. This chapter discusses what those are, so your Yorkie can live securely and happily with you in your home.

How to Prepare Your Home for Your Yorkie

The best way you can prepare your home prior to your Yorkie's arrival is dog-proofing it. This will keep it safe by preventing access to any dangerous or hazardous areas and items.

Yorkies love to explore their surroundings, and often this will involve sniffing, pulling, and chewing items that they find.

Set up boundaries in your house where you do not want your Yorkie to be left to its own devices.

How to Set Up A Safe Space for Your Yorkie

The key to creating a safe space for your Yorkie is to evaluate areas in your home where it can get in trouble. As you go from one space to another, assess what your Yorkie might do there. Are there any items that can attract its attention and it will start gnawing on? Drop to ground level and get a perspective on how your Yorkie sees its surroundings.

Here are some of the things to watch out for:

- **Nooks and crannies.** There could be crevices or holes where your Yorkie can squeeze itself and get stuck. It is best to have these covered or repaired.

- **Electrical wires and cables.** Your tiny Yorkie could get tangled in loose electrical wires and cables lying around. You can tuck cords behind furniture or lift them high enough out of your Yorkie's reach. Wind up any excess cord length.

- **Loose and hanging objects.** You will need to fix wobbly or unsteady furniture, or else it may topple down on your Yorkie. Hanging tablecloths may get pulled, and the things sitting on top of the table might fall on your dog. Keep these things away from your dog's reach. Dog repellent sprays, a harmless solution that tastes awful to dogs, can be sprayed on items in your home to keep your Yorkie away from them.

- **Yard.** Do a thorough sweep around your yard and cover any holes and gaps, store garden supplies and woodpiles.

- **Swimming pool/pond.** If you have a swimming pool, keep a close lookout on your Yorkie when it is near the vicinity. It may slip and fall into the water. Although it can doggy paddle, it usually does not have enough stamina to navigate itself to reach safety, and could end up drowning. If you have a pond, keep your Yorkie away from it. Algae growing in the pond can be toxic to your dog.

- **Personal belongings.** If you have expensive shoes, clothes and children's toys, remember to store these out of reach.

Hazardous Items to Keep Out of Your Yorkie's Reach

There are everyday objects we use that are harmful to Yorkies. A rule of thumb is always to keep them away and do not let you Yorkie have access to them. Identify where the chemical hazards in your home are located and clear them away.

Some plants are poisonous to Yorkies such as aloe vera and ivy. If you have these in your home, keep them away from your Yorkie.

Here are some products that you need to store and lock, so your Yorkie cannot reach them:

- Cleaning solutions such as laundry detergents, bleach, air freshener, etc.

- Hygiene products such as shampoo, soap, lotion, medicine, etc.

- Car products such as motor oil, antifreeze, etc. (be especially careful with antifreeze. A small amount of the solution can permanently melt a dog's kidney in just an hour).

- Gardening solutions such as fertilizer, insecticide, etc.

- Plants that are poisonous to Yorkies include aloe vera, ivy, jade, dumb cane, etc. (check the Yorkie Foundation's list of potentially poisonous plants to dogs).

Introducing Your Yorkie to Your Family – How Should You do It?

Upon seeing your Yorkie when bringing it home for the first time, your family may get overly excited and won't be able to wait their turn to cuddle the dog. Before your Yorkie comes to your home, you need to set rules regarding how your family should approach the dog.

Orient your family on the proper way to pick up, hold and set down a Yorkie. Doing this will teach them how to correctly and safely handle the dog. This is especially important if it is still a pup. Like a newborn babe, a puppy's body is fragile and sensitive. If handled roughly it may cause the pup to feel anxiety, pain, and soreness.

Once the initial introductions are done, allow your Yorkie to calm down and explore the house. When you see it starting to get comfortable, you may allow your family to spend more time with the dog.

You should also set rules during the Yorkie's meal time, especially if you have kids. Do not allow your children to disturb your Yorkie while it is eating. It might get agitated when it gets disturbed during meal time and could bite your kids.

Everyone in the family can also help in taking care of the Yorkie by setting a plan and schedule. You can designate different responsibilities, such as grooming, feeding, training and taking it out for walks.

Since the Yorkie is such a tiny dog, everyone must be careful not to step on or trip over it. Yorkies are fragile dogs, and accidents like these can cause serious injuries.

Bringing a Rescued Yorkie Home

Bringing a rescued Yorkie home is essentially the same as one that is bought from a breeder. This means you will need to prepare basic supplies. However, remember that being a rescue dog could somehow affect its behavior.

Gradually introduce it to the spaces in your home, the toys it can play with, and the items it will use. Give it some time to feel comfortable, and never force anything on the dog. It can take one to two months before your Yorkie becomes fully adjusted to your home. After this stage, you can begin to take it out for walks and to visit new places.

Rescued dogs are prone to exhibit fearful behavior such as shaking, retreating, and excessive barking in response to stimuli that distress them or remind them of unfavorable experiences. These include loud noises, car rides, being picked up by strangers without a proper introduction, and walking in crowded areas.

Never force your Yorkie to be exposed to such stimuli and situations. If these things must become part of your dog's life, slowly introduce them to your dog's environments. An example is having to go to the dog park for exercise. During the first day spend five minutes in the park and see how the dog responds. If it responds positively, you can gradually increase the time it spends in the dog park, until it is comfortable and unapprehensive. Another option would be to carry your Yorkie in a carrier or pet stroller if you need to move from one place to another.

Family Members, Children, and Other Pets – How Can You Help Your Yorkie Adjust?

It helps your Yorkie adjust to its new home and family when you establish a routine. You can do this by setting a specific time and person for a particular activity. Meals should be served at the same time every day by the same person; walks should be consistent daily and be done by the one who was assigned to do so. This is also the same case for bonding and play time.

If you have other pets in the house, the key is to introduce them to one another slowly. You can do this by placing the existing pet first in its cage or crate. Allow your Yorkie to approach the cage and see how they respond to each other. After 30 minutes, allow your existing pet to approach your Yorkie.

Initial introductions must always be supervised, especially if your existing pet is a larger dog. There is a chance they will be hostile to each other, at the start. There might be a few brawls, but they will eventually work things out, as long as no one gets hurt.

Show the same affection to the existing pet as you do to your new Yorkie. Also, provide each pet its own food and water bowl so they will not be fighting with each other over it. Initially place each pets' dishes at a distance until they are comfortable with each other and can eat together.

CHAPTER 6

Yorkie Pet Supplies – What Does Your Dog Need?

You would not want to find yourself running to a store because you need a specific item to help you in responding to your Yorkie's needs. This chapter discusses the necessary items you or your Yorkie will directly use, such as a grooming kit, dog bed, harness, and leash.

Yorkie Grooming Kit – What Should You Have?

The Yorkshire Terrier is a breed that demands a lot in the grooming department. Whether you are aiming for show-quality locks or an easy-to-maintain cut, you will need to get these essential grooming supplies.

Whether you are aiming for show-quality locks or an easy-to-maintain cut for your Yorkie, you will need to get essential grooming supplies.

Yorkie Grooming Tools

- Shampoo/soap and conditioner for Yorkshire Terriers
- Hairbrush and comb for dogs
- Spritz/coat spray – this will help protect it from contact friction and the elements
- Towel for drying your Yorkie after baths
- Cotton swabs for cleaning the eyes and ears
- Toothbrush/finger brush for small dog
- Dog toothpaste

Yorkie Grooming Comb and Brush

Brushing a Yorkie's coat is essential because it distributes the natural oil that it produces all over its body. It also prevents the Yorkie's hair from becoming frizzy and matted. You will need the right tools to achieve a healthy and neat coat for your Yorkie.

Combs

Combing usually prepares the coat before brushing, by separating the hairs.

A good set of combs will include these three types:

- Basic over-all body comb that you will use before brushing
- Small facial comb to use over the face and ears. This can also be used on the paws.
- De-matting comb to fix tangles that cannot be straightened with a regular comb

For Yorkies with closely shaved coats, you can use the over-all body comb and run it through its body. Be sure to buy combs that are good quality that will not rust, warp or bend.

Brushes

The ideal type to get is a pin brush. However, take note of the pin quality, as this can affect your Yorkie's coat.

A brush with high-quality pins will not bend or push back into the cushion. If the brush you are using does this, it is time to get a new one. The ends of the pins must also be of superior quality as this is the part that makes contact with the Yorkie's skin. Choose a brush that is appropriately-sized for your Yorkie. This will allow you to reach spots easily while making it comfortable for the dog.

For Yorkies with long show coats, a boar bristle brush is an ideal type to use. Boar bristle brush will effectively distribute the dog's natural oil all over its coat, making it smooth and shiny.

Yorkie Trimmer

It is imperative that you use the right trimmer or clippers for your Yorkie. Using the wrong one will make it difficult to trim its coat, or worse, cause injuries. If you think human clippers can do the job, they will eventually wear down because it is being used on the wrong type of hair. Pet clippers for dogs have a more powerful motor that stays cool when used for a long time.

Here are the types of blades that are ideal to use for your clippers when grooming your Yorkie:

- **No. 4 Blade.** The rule of thumb for clipper blades is the lower the number, the longer the hair will be cut. This type of blade is best if you are aiming for a puppy cut. It will leave the hair an inch long and will also be fine to use all over the dog's body (except the head and feet).

- **No. 7 and No. 7F Blade.** This is good for refining the Yorkie's puppy cut. It will cut the hair slightly shorter than the No. 4 blade and can be used on the dog's chest and abdomen. The No. 7 blade is skip-toothed and has coarse, uneven teeth that are useful for eliminating matted fur. No. 7F is comprised of even teeth that leaves the coat leveled and smooth. To get the best results from using this blade, brush the Yorkie's fur first.

- **No. 10 Blade.** It gives an even shorter cut than the No.7 blade. This is useful for trimming edges, especially around the chin, backs of the legs, face, and ears. Make sure that your Yorkie is calm and comfortable before trimming its face, and slowly and carefully cut its hair to avoid injuries.

Yorkie Shampoo and Yorkie Soap – What is the Best One to Use for Your Dog?

Since the Yorkie's skin is sensitive, it is always best to seek your veterinarian's advice for the most suitable shampoo you can use on your dog. A good rule of thumb is to use one that is gentle and fragrance-free. Shampoos with natural components, such as coconut oil, essential oils, and oatmeal, work best.

A good rule of thumb for Yorkie Shampoos is to use one that is gentle and fragrance-free.

Never use human shampoo on your Yorkie. The pH balance for humans and dogs are different, and human shampoos do not address what your Yorkie's coat needs. Using the wrong shampoo can lead to dryness, irritation, and poor quality of the coat.

A good shampoo for your Yorkie should be able to do the following:

- **Moisturize.** Shampoos with ingredients like almond oil can usually help achieve this. This will help prevent dryness.
- **Calming.** Ingredients with oatmeal can help calm your Yorkie's skin and provide relief when it is already suffering from skin dryness. Other calming ingredients include eucalyptus, peppermint, and tea tree oil.

On the other hand, here are some ingredients to avoid:

- **Parabens.** Can cause hormonal imbalance
- **Petroleum.** Can impede the secretion of the dog's natural oil
- **Sodium lauryl sulfate.** Can irritate the dog's eyes

Yorkie Puppy Shampoo - What are Safe Ones for Your Baby Yorkie?

You should take double the amount of caution when choosing a shampoo for a baby Yorkie. Stay away from ones that have artificial fragrance. This is also not the right stage of the puppy's life to use medicated shampoos like anti-tick and flea. A mild and natural cleansing shampoo works best for Yorkie puppies.

Walking with Your Yorkie – What do You Need?

There are a couple of things that you will need when you take your Yorkie out for a walk. These include:

- Harness/collar
- Leash

The right size and type will bring many benefits for you and your Yorkie. It will allow you to have a firm control when you lead the dog beside you. It will also prevent any injuries to which Yorkies are prone to when using a collar (explained further in the following section "Yorkie Dog Collar").

Yorkie Harness

Collars are generally used during walks for other breeds, but not for the Yorkie. A harness is ideal to use for walks with a Yorkie as it distributes the tension all over its body. This will not put pressure on the Yorkie's throat when it pulls.

*A harness is ideal to use for walks with a Yorkie
as it distributes the tension all over its body.*

You can choose among the different types of harness:

- **Strap harness.** It is positioned on the dog using buckles.
- **Wrap/vest harness.** It is donned on like a vest, with the connector for the leash on the upper back.

The strap and wrap harness both have room for a collar, so your Yorkie can still wear it for identification. Harnesses that can be fastened using Velcro flaps or nylon straps will make it easier to wear for your Yorkie. A good quality harness must be durable, weather resistant, and washable. Harnesses with nylon webbing are the best choice to endure the elements while being breathable and light.

It would be ideal to measure your Yorkie's size before shopping for a harness. You may not immediately find one that can instantly fit your Yorkie but choosing one that is adjustable will give it a snug fit. Use the harness only when you are out exercising your Yorkie; prolonged wear can get your Yorkie's hair tangled.

Yorkie Dog Collar

Collars attached on the leash, usually put pressure on the dog's trachea. When your Yorkie lunges or pulls, the tension and force are on its neck. This usually brings harm, particularly to small dogs as they have lesser muscular support which makes them prone to trachea collapse. This condition will be painful for your Yorkie and may require surgery to treat.

This is why collars with tags should only be used for identification purposes.

The ideal collar for your Yorkie should be durable while being lightweight. Nylon collars work best compared to leather, which will wear down and rip when constantly exposed to moisture.

If you plan to buy a collar for your Yorkie puppy that it will use for a long time, an ideal width is 0.47 in. (1.2 cm.). Regularly check it for adjustments, at least once a week. You will know that your Yorkie's collar has a good fit if you can slip two of your fingers through it and the neck.

Yorkie Dog Leash

Here are some things you need to consider when getting a leash for your Yorkie:

- **Length.** An ideal measurement is 4 to 6 ft. (122 to 183 cm.). A narrow width will be good as this will be light on your Yorkie's back. A retractable leash is also optional to give your Yorkie more freedom to move around in wider landscapes but be sure that it undergoes obedience training first before using this type of leash.

- **Clip.** This is the part of the leash that attaches to the harness. Stainless steel is a good material to choose, as it does not rust.

- **Durability.** Make sure it is made of a material that can withstand the elements (especially rain). This is the only thing that holds you and your Yorkie. You do not want your dog to dart off, because of a cheap leash that ripped apart. A good material for leashes is nylon. Never use a chain leash for your Yorkie, as this material can cause injuries.

- **Comfort and safety.** If you can, you may want to test the leash on your Yorkie before purchasing it. See how the dog moves around with it and how it feels in your hands.

You may also consider buying two leashes so the other one will serve as a back-up in case the primary leash gets damaged. Buying a slightly bigger backup leash will assure you are prepared, once you Yorkie grows to adulthood.

You may want to skip decorative trinkets, like tassels or beads that some leashes have. They can fall off, and/or your Yorkie will chew on them and could choke.

If you have a Yorkie that participates in dog shows, a martingale collar is commonly used to showcase the dog's full physique, with minimal obstructions to the appearance.

Making Your Yorkie Comfortable – What does Your Dog Need?

Part of giving your Yorkie the care it needs is making it comfortable. There are some items you need to provide, as explained in the following sections.

Yorkie Dog Beds

Letting your Yorkie rest on a cozy bed will protect it from long-term skeletal and muscular injuries. The bed must be able to mold around your dog's body and evenly distribute its weight. Some areas of the coat of your Yorkie's body may recede, make the skin even more sensitive, and make it difficult for the hair to regrow.

A dog bed is especially necessary when your Yorkie comes into its senior years. Many senior dogs who did not have a proper sleeping cushion when they were younger may develop osteoarthritis. This condition makes it difficult for senior dogs to lie down, rise, and walk around.

A bed also provides security to your Yorkie when you are out. It contributes to a den-like atmosphere which can help it calm down when separation anxiety sets in.

Here are some types of dog beds that can work well with your Yorkie:

- **Bolster bed.** The bottom is thickly cushioned. Its sides are raised a bit, with one side open, so the dog can easily fit inside. It works great for Yorkie puppies as it provides the most warmth out of all the types.

- **Mattress.** This is a generic flatbed with no raised sides. If you have observed your Yorkie loves to lie on the floor, this type can be a good match.

Whatever type of bed you choose, make sure it is washable. You can also opt to have a bed cover to make clean-up easier and to wash the bed only a few times.

Yorkie Dog Carrier

The Yorkie's tiny size makes it one of the easiest dogs to carry around. Having a dedicated carrier will make transport even easier and safer for you and your Yorkie.

Another side to the Yorkie's size is it can only walk so far before all its energy is exhausted. Placing it in a carrier will save its energy when you have reached your destination.

A carrier will also protect it from getting tripped over or stepped on. This is especially important if you are traversing in a crowded area. Although you can easily carry your Yorkie in your arms, should the need arise for you to use both of your hands, a carrier will give you more freedom to be more mobile.

Here are some types of bags that can work as carriers for your Yorkie:

- **Sling bag.** This type is designed to hang near your body and strapped over your shoulders. It has a pocket that is deep enough to nestle your Yorkie at the same time allowing it to poke its head out to breathe and see the surroundings. Some sling bags have a meshed zipped covering which can be a good option if your Yorkie tends to jump. You can choose any design that suits your taste, but the most important thing to consider is it must be durable, especially its stitching. Also, make sure it is washable and easy to clean, in case your Yorkie has an accident inside. A good sling bag size is 9 in (height) x 7.5 in (width) x 11.5 in (length) (22.86 x 19.05 x 29.21 cm.).

- **Carrier bag.** This type has firmer sides and is more structured. It provides more security and room, compared to a sling bag. A good carrier bag size is 9 in (height) x 9 in (width) x 15 in (length) (23 x 23 x 38 cm.)

- **Strollers.** Think carrier bags with wheels. It works the same as a baby stroller and has a covering that will shield your Yorkie from the sun. If you do not want to lift all that weight that using a sling or carrier bag demands, this is your best choice. Make sure you use a stroller with wheels that can glide easily on different surfaces.

Yorkie Dog Crate

If you need to travel a farther distance and are traveling via plane or ship, then a dog crate is imperative. A crate is also needed for locations with regulations that dogs must be in a crate for the safety of the public.

Crates can be built of wire or plastic. Wire crates provide more airflow and can allow your dog to view its surroundings. It is also easier to clean up. Wire crates also work better when crate training your Yorkie. However, the wire crate can be noisy when your dog's nails clang against it. On the other hand, plastic crates are ideal for plane travel. They are sturdier and offer more privacy for your Yorkie.

Be sure to choose one that has enough space in which to place its food and water bowl. A crate that has a length of 18 to 22 in. (45.72 to 55.88 cm.) would comfortably house most adult Yorkies.

Yorkie Dog House

Dog houses are typically used to shelter dogs who must stay outside the house. Yorkies are very much indoor dogs. This breed is sensitive and should stay indoors. Providing them with their own area where they can have some privacy and lie down comfortably, would oftentimes suffice.

If you insist on providing your Yorkie with a dog house, it will only be to fortify its privacy and give it a space to retreat to within its own tiny four walls. A structured dog house is not needed anymore; a soft-walled enclosure that gives a cozy atmosphere is adequate.

It can have the same size as the crate and should be big enough to position its dog bed in a corner. Remember to clean its dog house regularly to prevent the build-up of bacteria.

Yorkie Dog Bowls – What You Need to Make Mealtime Easy and Mess-free for Your Yorkie

You may not put much thought into the type of dish your Yorkie will eat from, but this is the most important item. Stainless steel is the best material for dog bowls. Since it is heavy, it will provide a sturdy foundation, and your Yorkie will not be able to move it when eating from the bowl. Steel bowls are also scratch-proof. Be sure to buy one that is rimmed with rubber, to make it stay in place.

Stay away from plastic dog bowls as these can get scratched, and it is in these cracks that bacteria can cultivate. Plastic bowls can easily topple over and send the food flying.

A shallow food bowl will make it easier for your Yorkie to eat. A bowl that is 4 to 6 in. (10.16 to 15.24 cm.) in diameter works best for small dogs like the Yorkie and will allow it to reach all its food.

When it comes to the water bowl, you may want one that you can install a water bottle, so it can dispense a constant supply. Ideally, your Yorkie's water must not come from the tap as it contains harmful chemicals like fluoride and chlorine. Some fancier water bowls come with the filtration system that ensures clean water and prevent it from getting stagnant.

Yorkie Dog Toys – What are the Different Types?

Yorkies are naturally playful dogs and love to play and have fun. Providing toys will keep it entertained and prevent boredom from setting in and escalating to destructive behavior.

Yorkie Puppy Chew Toys

As a Yorkie puppy grows, its teeth will start to emerge. This stage will often cause pain to its gums and will make your Yorkie puppy want to gnaw on something. To avoid your shoes and other personal belongings becoming the outlet, you will need to provide chew toys.

Chew toys can also help maintain your Yorkie's dental health. Dental chew toys can reduce the build-up of plaque and bad breath. Your Yorkie will need all the teeth-strengthening and cleaning it can get.

Chew toys for puppies must be soft enough that they will not damage their teeth but must also be durable that they will not chip-off and get ingested. The particles that break off from the chew toy might become choking hazards to your Yorkie.

Stay away from cheap plastic toys that are BPA-laden. This material is harmful to your Yorkie's health. Do not buy toys that have squeakers in them, as your Yorkie might choke on them if it manages to tear the toy apart.

If you notice that the toy has blood spots when your Yorkie is playing with it, or you observe symptoms of diarrhea, vomiting, or loss of appetite, immediately dispose of the toy.

Remember to buy the right size. Chew toys that are too small might choke your Yorkie, while ones that are too big might strain its jaw.

Yorkie Exercise and Enrichment Toys

Enrichment toys will stimulate your Yorkie more and will be a lot more interesting and fun. Some of these toys include puzzles where it needs to use its sense of smell to solve them. When your Yorkie successfully figures out the puzzle the toy will dispense a treat. These toys also develop your Yorkie's dexterity, balance, and coordination.

Yorkie Accessories

Accessories for your Yorkie can provide practical benefits as well as aesthetic value. Here are some accessories you may want your Yorkie to wear.

Yorkie Dog Clothes

If you live in a cooler climate area, you may want your Yorkie to wear apparel like sweaters and jackets, to help keep him warm. Since Yorkies lack undercoats, they have little natural defense against the cold. However, if you live in warmer climates like in tropical countries, you may want to have it wear something light, breathable, and just enough to protect it from the rays and heat of the sun.

If you live in an area where the climate is cooler, you may want your Yorkie to wear apparel like sweaters and jackets.

If your Yorkie is suffering from a skin condition, clothes can also protect it from being exposed.

It is important to train your Yorkie to wear clothes when it is still young and can become used to it. You may have noticed dogs writhing with discomfort when something is clad on their bodies.

To find the right clothes that will fit your Yorkie, measure the following parts:

- Neck where the collar will be positioned
- Chest – take the tape measure around the chest, just behind its front legs
- Back – measure from the base of the neck up to the base of the tail

Although the Yorkie will typically fall under the small and medium size, getting these measurements will give it a more accurate fit. The most important thing is your Yorkie will be able to move around, and the clothes must not constrict its body.

You may also consider letting your Yorkie wear shoes. This will keep its paws from directly contacting scorching roads or icy ground. It can also keep its paws clean by avoiding contact with mud or puddles. To get the right shoe size for your Yorkie, you can outline its paw on a piece of paper and measure the width and length with a tape measure.

The design of the clothes and shoes will be completely up to your taste and preferences. Just remember that whatever you pick must be comfortable for your Yorkie.

Yorkie Hair Products

Yorkies who are groomed to compete in dog shows usually have the hair on their heads clipped with a bow. Other accessories for Yorkies include jewelry, sunglasses, and hats.

Yorkies who are groomed to compete in dog shows usually have the hair on their heads clipped with a bow.

These items make your Yorkie more fashionable. It is fun to dress up and accessorize your Yorkie but be careful not to overdo it to the point where movement is impeded.

Yorkie Dog Gate – Does Your Dog Need One?

A dog gate can provide various benefits for your Yorkie. It can set up a boundary to areas in your house where you do not want your dog to enter. If you have other pets, it can serve as a division to

give the animals some time out or keep them separated if either of them is injured or sick.

Here are some things to consider when buying and installing a pet gate for your Yorkie:

- Never place a dog gate on top of the stairs.
- Only buy a dog gate that is dog-proof and child-proof. The locks, slots, pinch points and screws can be hazardous if they manage to unhinge these mechanisms. A safe dog gate should also have a child-safety latch.
- Be sure that the gaps are not too wide that your Yorkie can squeeze itself and potentially get stuck.
- To make access easier for you, a dog gate that can swing open works well.

Yorkshire Terrier Snacks – What Can You Give Your Dog?

Snack and treats are essential for positive reinforcement when training your Yorkie. The quality of snacks you give should be screened. The best treats are easy to digest and made of natural ingredients. Be careful to exclude treats made of fillers and extenders. They must also be small enough for your Yorkie to chew on them easily.

Be cautious of treats that came from overseas. There has been an incident where dog treats from China were linked to causing Falconi syndrome, a condition that affects the dog's kidneys. These products were ordered to be taken down from shelves, but there are still some that remain in the market. Take a close look at the country in which it was made. Many products that have come from Asia have triggered allergic reactions in Yorkies.

There are some detrimental ingredients that are mixed in dog treats that causes dry skin, irritation, rashes, thinning hair, diarrhea and vomiting in Yorkies. Among these ingredients include artificial preservatives such as BHA, BHT, calcium propionate, potassium sorbate and sodium nitrate; artificial coloring, chemical humectants, and artificial sweeteners.

Never give your Yorkie treats made from rawhide. It used to be a popular option for owners to give to their dogs but has caused choking, and stomach and intestinal blockage. Some rawhides even contain formaldehyde and arsenic, which are deposited during manufacturing.

Dog treats for your Yorkie do not have to be shaped into little bones and smell like ham for them to be appealing. In fact, snacks are a great way to supplement the fruit and vegetable intake of your dog.

CHAPTER 7

How to Take Care of a Yorkie – Yorkie Care 101

A Yorkie demands a regular and delicate grooming routine. Neglecting any hygiene habit can escalate into a worse situation before you know it. Its hair can easily get matted, which can affect the coat and skin's overall condition. Grooming also benefits your Yorkie's health and can prevent certain conditions from setting in.

Grooming Your Yorkie

This routine is vital in keeping your Yorkie's appearance neat and healthy. Grooming even takes a notch up if you have your Yorkie compete in dog shows. Whatever lifestyle your Yorkie has, grooming benefits are the same for all dogs of this breed.

It can help avoid health issues like candidiasis, dermatitis, and other skin diseases. During grooming time, you will be able to individually and closely check your Yorkie's parts. This will let you see if there are any indicators of sickness, and let you take action immediately.

Bathing frequency depends on how long your Yorkie's coat is. Show Yorkies must be groomed weekly. Yorkies with shorter coats can be bathed once every three weeks or so unless they get muddy or otherwise very dirty. If your Yorkie has more sensitive skin than normal, you may need to lessen the frequency of its bath. Always check with your veterinarian if this is the case.

Yorkie Hair Care

Your Yorkie may initially resist your efforts in combing its hair. Be gentle with your strokes and never push the dog when it struggles. You can create a positive association to this by giving it treats when it behaves, during brushing time.

After brushing its coat, you may want to spritz it with a leave-in spray to seal in the quality of hair after brushing. This will help prevent breakage and split ends, especially when you drybrush your Yorkie. Neglecting the onset of split ends can make the rest of the hair frayed and unhealthy. This is also a good step in maintaining your Yorkie's hair and smell, until its next bath time. Never settle for a low-quality cheap spray, as it can block your Yorkie's pores and will make the coat feel pasty.

When you are in the spritzing stage of your Yorkie's grooming routine, start at the roots and spray as you go, while brushing its coat to distribute the product all the way to the tips evenly. If your Yorkie sports a show coat, you may want to spray just a half of a hair section and sweep it with a brush. You can repeat the process and give it a quick spritz daily. You can also spray some of the product directly in your hands and apply it on your Yorkie.

Yorkshire Terrier Long Hair

A method of brushing a show Yorkie's coat is line brushing. It involves separating the hair into strips. This allows you to comb each layer, and not to miss an area of your Yorkie's coat.

Below are the steps for line brushing:

1. Make your Yorkie feel calm and have it lie on its side.
2. Starting from the lower portion of the body, take a greyhound comb and gently brush the coat up and separate the hair. Make horizontal lines that will make the skin visible.
3. Starting on the line from step 2, go over the hair below the line with the comb until it can glide all the way through easily.
4. Create a new strip from the previous one and simply repeat the process, until you have gone through the entire coat.

Yorkshire Terrier Short Hair

For Yorkies with a short coat, a small slicker brush that is of superior quality will work great in de-matting its fur, to produce a softer and neater coat.

Before doing any brushing, you must check your Yorkie's coat for mats. Matting happens when the fur gets tangled and forms clumps. The Yorkie's fur is prone to matting, so make sure you regularly check if there is any present. Should you see one that is too thick, you will need to go to a pet groomer, to have it safely removed.

If there are no signs of matted fur, you can take your slicker brush and sweep it along the direction of the coat's growth. Be careful only to apply a few strokes, as repeatedly going over the same spot may cause the skin to become irritated.

Taking a greyhound comb, sweep it gently all over the coat so you can detect any mats that are still hiding. De-matting shampoos and sprays are available on the market to make this process easier.

If you see that your Yorkie is wincing in pain when you try to force the comb on a mat, you may have to go to the pet groomer to have it safely shaved off.

To avoid the formation of mats, comb your Yorkie with the slicker brush every three days. You may need to be gentler on your Yorkie's groin area and armpits.

Different Types of Yorkie Haircuts

Letting your Yorkie sport a specific haircut will reflect on the type of lifestyle it leads and activity it does. Some styles will be easier for you to maintain, while one type is the required type for dog shows.

*Letting your Yorkie sport a specific haircut will reflect
on the type of lifestyle it leads and activity it does.*

- **Show groom.** This is usually the style Yorkies have and are required in show competitions. It showcases the Yorkie's beautiful flowing long coat, and skirts around their paws. Even if your Yorkie does not participate in dog shows you can still have it sport this style. Just remember that you will have to establish a grooming routine to maintain it.

- **Outline groom.** This cut is similar to the show groom. The only difference is that the head and mustache are trimmed shorter, and the coat skirt is clipped short that it sits above floor level.

- **Teddy bear/Puppy cut.** If you do not want to deal with constantly combing your Yorkie's coat, the puppy cut is the option for you. It leaves a ¾-inch length of the coat while leaving the chest hair longer so that it looks like a bib. This look is reminiscent of when the Yorkie is still a puppy.

- **Kennel cut.** The coat is cut very short but still leaving a bit of length on the legs, tail, and head. The mustache and ears are also carefully cut to about ½ inch length. The hair on the paws is also cut short. This is the best cut for hot climate and summer months.

- **Schnauzer trim.** The cut is fashioned to look like a Schnauzer. This is done by keeping the mustache longer and leaving the body's bottom and legs 1/3 of a length of the hair. This creates an appearance of a skirt. The upper portion is cut to ½ inch, and also leaves ½ inch of length on the chest to also create a bib look.

Maintaining Your Yorkie's Nails

You will need to check the nail length every two to three months. Even if you fail to look at them closely, you will know that your Yorkie's nails are starting to grow longer when it makes clacking sounds as it moves across the floor.

You may opt to go to a pet groomer for this. However, if you insist on cutting your Yorkie's nails yourself, first you need to get a pair of good quality nail trimmers. There is also a nail grinder variety available, which files the dog's nails instead of cutting them.

If you are using a trimmer, you need to locate your Yorkie's quick that is inside the nail. The quick is the cuticle that holds the vein and blood vessels. Accidentally cutting the quick will cause pain and bleeding, which can lead to infections.

Start by cutting the nail on the tips and go further in slowly, a little bit a time. Check how close you are nearing the quick and stop when you see the pinkish or gray cuticle. You may want to file it to give a smoother finish. A little tip: it is easier to cut your Yorkie's nails after bath time as water can moisten the nails and make them softer.

How to Keep Ticks and Fleas Away

Since Yorkies are short, this makes their body more exposed to the ground. This allows ticks and fleas to infest your Yorkie's coat more easily. Yorkies with long coats can pick up fleas and ticks quicker and will be harder to spot them when they have set in their bodies.

Examine your Yorkie's body for fleas and ticks at least once a day. Watch out for any small black specks. Common areas where they tend to hide are the armpits, head, ears, back, and stomach. You may also want to run a flea comb through the coat since its fine bristles can trap fleas and ticks that are sticking to the coat and skin. Comb through the head first and move on to the back, legs, and lastly the stomach. Slowly and gently sweep the flea comb across your Yorkie's body, lest it will cause cuts, due to the comb's fine tips. After every few strokes, slide your finger across the comb's tips under running water and soap. Doing this will drown the fleas and ticks.

If your Yorkie already has a bad flea and tick infestation, you may want to use a medicated shampoo specifically formulated to kill the pests. Be sure to choose one with organic ingredients, and stay away from harsh chemical products, as these can cause seizures in dogs. Lather all of the external areas of its body and rinse them well. Be sure to wash its towel often, so the ticks and fleas will not stay trapped in it.

Natural herbal sprays, like rosemary and citronella, also work to ward off ticks and fleas. This chemical-free option will not only save your Yorkie from tick and flea infestation but also leave it smelling pleasant. Be sure to spritz it on your Yorkie's fur, before heading outside.

You will also need to clean and vacuum your home thoroughly. Be sure to throw out the filter bags and rinse the canister with hot water to disinfect it to kill any eggs that may remain.

Yorkie Puppy Care – What You Need to Know

Puppyhood is the Yorkie's most fragile state. They start out in life as tiny pups in need of their mother's protection and nutrition. Your role will be to supplement the mother's care in areas where she may lack.

Newborn Yorkies weigh around 2 to 20 gm. (0.07 to 0.70 oz.) and should be gaining weight as the days pass. Be vigilant on how the puppy's weight progresses, and if you see any signs of it reducing instead of increasing weight, you need to have your veterinarian check it right away.

The mother's milk will be the puppy Yorkie's primary source of nutrition. You can help the dam produce milk with rich nutrition, by feeding it with high-quality food. Be sure always to have fresh water accessible to her.

More or less the dam's maternal instinct will take over, and she will nurse and clean her pups. You will just need to observe how things are going. You may need to step in when the mother gets sick or rejects her pups, a puppy constantly gets pushed away by its littermates and does not have the chance to suckle or is too weak to feed. In cases like this, you may need to bottle feed the pup. It is imperative that you check with your veterinarian on what milk to give your Yorkie puppies.

At around week three you may see the puppies' eyes start to open and start to move around. Their sense of smell has already started to develop, so this makes it a prime time to introduce it to potty training. Lay newspapers around its whelping area where it can potty. It will be able to familiarize itself with the scent and will know which spot it needs to urinate or defecate in.

By the start of week four or five, the Yorkie puppies may now be able to eat solid food. House training can also be started at this early age. In this stage, you should start letting the pups get accustomed to being touched by humans. It is also best if they will be made comfortable with being touched on the mouth, teeth, and paws. This will prove important when brushing its teeth and trimming its nails.

When the Yorkie pup has grown to a few months old, you should start discipline training. Puppy-proof areas in your house where it could get lost or stuck. Always have fresh water nearby and develop a consistent feeding routine.

Senior Yorkies – How to Take Care of Your Yorkshire Terrier in its Old Age

Caring for a senior Yorkie may be a bittersweet stage for you and your pet. You would look back to all the years you have been together and do all that you can to let it feel extra loved in the later part of its life. You need to know what may happen to a senior Yorkie, so you can anticipate any response that may be appropriate.

It is safe to assume that if it has reached 8 to 12 years old, it has entered this stage. You may start to see signs of slowing down, physical limitations, reduced activity, and more vulnerability to sickness.

Senior Yorkies may need to have more frequent visits to the veterinarian for geriatric check-ups.

Senior Yorkies may need to have more frequent visits to the veterinarian for check-ups. This is essential, so you will be able to spot any onset of medical issues before they worsen. Some medical procedures that may be done are blood count, urinalysis, chemistry panel, stool testing and X-rays.

As much as possible, maintain your exercise routine with your Yorkie, and keep it mobile. Unless it experiences pain, or is unable to carry on, help it to remain active. Your Yorkie may need more water breaks at this stage, so provide it with water when necessary. It is ideal to have a break every five minutes. If you are used to having walking sessions for 30 minutes, you may break it down at different times of the day to allow your senior Yorkie to rest in between. Your senior Yorkie may also need more protection from the elements more than ever. Provide him with warm apparel during the cold season, and clothes that can shield him from the sun's rays and heat during hot summer months.

You may notice that your Yorkie has a decreased appetite in older age. If you have fed it with high-quality dog food, continue to do so. Should there be a drastic change in its weight and appearance (thin and bony), immediately check with your veterinarian for a suitable meal plan to maintain a healthy weight. Also check with him or her if your senior Yorkie may need supplements, especially for joint health. Do a routine inspection of its body by running your hand over it and checking for any lumps and bumps.

The skin will be more sensitive during this period or may even develop bald spots. If so it is vital to use high quality and gentle products, that will not cause irritation or any skin issues.

Your senior Yorkie may take naps more frequently than when it was younger. Let your family know about this to respect its resting times, and not force it to play or engage in strenuous activities. This is also a time to give him a dog bed if you have not already done so, as it can properly support its body.

Senior Yorkies may be disoriented if frequent changes in your house occur. They may have a difficult time locating certain items and spots. Their vision and hearing may have been affected by old age, so it is best to help it not have a hard time by keeping things consistent.

Yorkie Exercise – How Much of it Does Your Dog Need?

The Yorkshire Terrier is an agile and active breed. It is through exercise that Yorkies can release their stored energy. If not exercised daily, your Yorkie will channel its energy into destructive behavior like excessive barking and chewing.

It requires regular exercise to maintain optimum health. Exercise is highly beneficial for its cardiovascular health, muscles, and metabolism. It is also a great way to be able to socialize with other dogs and humans.

Your Yorkie needs both moderate exercise and more intense cardiovascular activities. Moderate exercise should include daily walks, but not to the point where it will leave your Yorkie panting heavily. It should be taken out for a walk at least once daily. It is essential to have a daily schedule, so it will understand that it is in this particular part of the day it will have some exercise.

The ideal duration of walking sessions for adolescents is between 15 to 20 minutes, while for fully grown adults it is 20 to 25 minutes. Keep it moderate and walk at a brisk pace. Always check with your Yorkie; a fast pace for you will leave your Yorkie behind. When you are in an open park, you can also allow your Yorkie to run free, but keep in mind that you need to supervise it.

If you are out of the house a good part of the day, walking your Yorkie before leaving will help it release some of its energy, and become calmer. Walks during the evening will help it have a better night's sleep. However, do not overdo it at this time, as it can make your Yorkie too awake to sleep. Remember to use a harness attached to a leash instead of a collar (explained in Chapter 6: Yorkie Pet Supplies, Walking Your Yorkie section).

Cardiovascular activities can be a game of fetch or a game of Frisbee.

Cardiovascular activities can be a game of fetch, or a game of Frisbee (please use a smaller disc that will enable your Yorkie to catch it easily). The important thing is your Yorkie should have short bursts of physical activity. This is ideally done once or twice a week.

How to Be a Yorkshire Terrier Savvy Owner

A Yorkie-savvy owner is more than one who provides food to the dog and take it out for walks but is also one who is knowledgeable about the breed. He or she knows the breed's history and understands how this can affect the dog's temperament. He or she also takes time to learn about possible medical conditions that the dog can acquire, and how to minimize the chances of that happening. He or she always consults with the veterinarian for any health issues, and what needs to be done for the dog.

The savvy Yorkie owner participates, or at least attends, dog shows that are breed-specific. He or she uses this time to connect with other Yorkie owners and lovers and seeks knowledge on things that can be learned about the breed. Nothing beats experience, and Yorkie owners will be happy to impart what they have to other aspiring breed owners.

CHAPTER 8

Housetraining Your Yorkie – What Skills does it Need to Know?

H ouse training is the most important phase in your Yorkie's young life, as it is going to live with you in your home. You do not want to be constantly cleaning after it, thus it is essential that your Yorkie learn where and when to do its business. Yorkies have a reputation for being hard to train, so it will require patience from you to succeed in this area. This chapter will cover tips and strategies to help you in housetraining your Yorkie.

What You Need to Know Before Housetraining Your Yorkie

Your Yorkie's age will give an idea how long it can hold its bladder. For example, if your Yorkie is two months old, it can only hold its bladder for two hours; three months for three hours and so on. By the eight month it will be able to hold for eight hours. This is the maximum time it can hold its bladder. However, this does not mean it will hold itself for this long.

If your Yorkie really needs to go potty, it will relieve itself, no matter how long it has been!

Obviously, the main reason your Yorkie relieves itself is when its bladder is full. However, there are instances where it urinates as a response to certain situations. This can be due to overexcitement, reaction to fear, incorrect housetraining, marking its territory, or a sign of a health concern.

You may want to start with a puppy pad when housetraining your Yorkie. Puppy or potty pads are absorbent rectangular mats, where your dog can step onto and do its business. Consider it as the "training wheels" of housebreaking, as this method is an easy way to get your Yorkie to relieve itself in a particular spot.

*Eventually, your Yorkie will need to graduate from
puppy pads and will move on to the outdoors.*

Eventually, your Yorkie will need to graduate from puppy pads and will move on to the outdoors. This will save you money and time since you will not constantly be buying the pads and cleaning the area where they are placed. Going outside will also allow your Yorkie to get some exercise and socialize with other animals.

How Can You and Your Yorkie Prepare for Housetraining?

Before beginning housetraining your Yorkie, you need to be well-equipped. Consider securing these following items:

- playpen
- tether
- puppy/potty pads
- newspapers
- cleaner to eliminate odor

Indoor or Outdoor – How Can You Train Your Yorkie to do its Business?

There may be some situations when you need to potty train your Yorkie inside, and also outside your home. Whatever the case may be, you need to keep in mind these common denominators:

1. **Choose a specific potty spot.** When your Yorkie shows signs that it needs to go, you need to bring it to this place. Never open your door to let your Yorkie out, and pick whatever area it will potty without any guidance. Doing this will make you miss out on valuable training opportunities and could

be dangerous for your Yorkie. When choosing a potty spot, keep in mind to take it some distance away from areas where family activities and food prep takes place. Ensure that your Yorkie can access this place at all times, including in different weather and seasons.

2. **Establish a routine.** Creating a familiar pattern for your Yorkie, for when and where it needs to go, will help it get accustomed to using this particular area. Letting your Yorkie approach this area after mealtime can be a good start to establishing this routine. This can also involve timing meals when you are around, so you can create a routine for going to the potty.

Essential Skills and Strategies for Yorkie Housetraining

It is crucial that you set rules to help expedite the success of this training.

1. Taking the tip from the previous section, stand in your chosen potty spot for your Yorkie and let it approach this area. Initially, it may take longer, and you may need to stay there for five to ten minutes. The best times to do this is 15 to 20 minutes after mealtime, after waking up, and when you arrive home. It takes about this much time for its bowel movements to kick in, so be patient.

2. Create a positive association to this act by praising and giving your Yorkie a treat when it has successfully done its business, in that particular area. The treat that you will use to reward your Yorkie should only be used when it has successfully acted.

3. When you see your Yorkie exhibiting signs that it needs to go potty, startle it by clapping your hands or making a loud sound. Then, immediately bring it to its potty spot.

Do's and Don'ts When Housetraining Your Yorkie

To make your house training sessions more effective, keep in mind these do's and don'ts:

DO'S

- Supervise in an enclosed area. This can be done if you erect a playpen where your Yorkie can stay, or you can also have it tethered by your side, using a harness and a leash.

- If you are using puppy pads, your Yorkie might start attacking and chewing them. You can place them in a canine litter box to keep it from being moved around. Unlike a cat litter box, canine litter boxes do not make use of sand.

- You may grow impatient when your Yorkie takes its time to potty, and if you do it may affect the training. Keep yourself occupied by using your mobile phone, etc. Remember that it can take between 15 to 20 minutes before your Yorkie is done with its business.

- Always watch out for signs when your Yorkie needs to go potty and be quick to respond to the situation. Signs may include lifting its leg, squatting, sniffing at a particular spot, and moving in circles.

DONT'S

- Do not enclose a Yorkie in a big area like an entire room (by locking it with a dog gate), or a small space like a crate when potty training. Leaving your Yorkie unsupervised in a big place can spell disaster for your floor, possessions and to the training altogether. A crate will not inhibit your Yorkie from relieving itself when it needs to go. Remember that you need to be with your Yorkie every step of the way.

- If you have already done its nightly potty routine, refrain from attending to it if it whines or barks. Letting your Yorkie undergo this process will help it learn to self-soothe, and not consistently seek your attention.

CHAPTER 9

Yorkshire Terrier Health and Nutrition

Your Yorkie's health is the most important thing you need be diligent about preserving. It is your responsibility to keep it at an optimum state. It is best to have a good understanding of possible medical issues, so you can take preventative measures. You will need to learn signs that signal the onset of these conditions and seek your veterinarian's advice before minor symptoms develop into something dangerous.

Yorkshire Terrier Life Span

A Yorkshire Terrier has an average lifespan of 12 to 15 years, with a median age of 13.5 years. Females live longer than males on average, by approximately 1.5 years.

Prolonging Your Yorkie's Life

There are some accidents that you can avoid, that could potentially save your Yorkie's life. Among these are preventing trauma. One scenario to remain watchful about is avoiding the possibility of your family members stepping on your Yorkie.

The pressure and weight pushed down on the dog are enough to kill them. In fact, trauma is the third leading cause of death for Yorkies and other small dogs. This is even more likelihood of fatality if trauma occurs when your Yorkie is a puppy.

You must inform everyone in your household to be careful where they are treading. A Yorkie can easily appear in any given spot, without attracting any attention. This is also especially important if one is going in on a darkened room where your Yorkie may be. Also, be sure when you sit down, your Yorkie isn't behind you!

Another situation that you should do your best to avoid is letting your Yorkie fall from too great a height. It may not be able to withstand the impact of a fall. This can happen when it is being mishandled, especially by children who can be rough with it, and who are not taught to hold a Yorkie properly. Your Yorkie can also fall from your hands if you are focusing on other things while carrying your Yorkie in your arms.

Be careful when opening doors where your Yorkie can quickly dart off to the road and can be possibly hit by a car. An unspayed female or unneutered male will have a higher tendency of escaping, as their hormones are driving them toward adventure! It is better to alert family members and guests upon their arrival, so you can place your Yorkie in a safe area, before opening the door.

These are some of the scenarios when obedience training is of utmost importance. When it has understood, and is capable of obeying commands such as "sit" and "come," you can control your Yorkie better.

Medical issues can be prevented from escalating to serious conditions, by taking your Yorkie to the veterinarian regularly and thinking preventatively. He or she will be able to give you an accurate prognosis, should your Yorkie have contracted some symptoms of potential illness. Chances of survival are always higher if you catch them before they worsen. You may want to consider setting aside funds that will cover your Yorkie's medical needs and treatments. Pet insurance is also available to cover health conditions such as infections, eye problems, allergies and skin problems, thyroid, and kidney diseases.

Yorkshire Terrier Health Concerns

Below are some of the top medical conditions that have caused high mortality rates in Yorkshire Terriers.

- **Parvovirus.** A fatal disease that infects the puppy's gastrointestinal tract and immune system. This can manifest in vomiting and diarrhea, which can quickly escalate to dehydration. Parvovirus is also highly contagious. Puppies become especially vulnerable during the period from when the antibodies from the mother's milk have decreased, but the vaccine has not yet come to full effect.

- **Distemper.** This is another highly contagious sickness that attacks the respiratory and/or gastrointestinal tract. Signs of distemper include coughing and weakness. If not immediately attended to, it can spread to the puppy's spinal cord and brain. A vaccine to combat this disease is available, and your Yorkie should get this shot. Avoid bringing your Yorkie outside until it has finished the series of this vaccine.

- **Leptospirosis.** This disease is commonly sourced from rodents and similar wildlife and can be transmitted to your Yorkie if it wades in puddles where a wild rodent urinated or defecated. This can quickly enter your Yorkie's system if it has cuts and abrasions. Signs your Yorkie has this disease are shivering, fever, muscle tenderness, dehydration, vomiting, diarrhea, and difficulty in breathing.

- **Respiratory Diseases.** Yorkies have high mortality rates, when they contract respiratory diseases, with 16.1% of infected Yorkies, dying from these. Some of the common respiratory conditions they can suffer from are pulmonary fibrosis, collapsed trachea, and Brachycephalic Airway Syndrome. When your Yorkie nears old age, gradual degeneration of lung condition can cause bronchitis.

- **Cancer.** Some forms of cancer Yorkies can have are lymphoma (tumor in the lymph nodes), skin cancer, cancer of the mammary gland, soft tissue sarcomas, and bone cancer.

- **Congenital disease.** These disorders are present when your Yorkie is born. One of the inherent disorders Yorkies can have is Portosystemic Shunts (PPS), also known as liver shunts. This condition inhibits blood from flowing to the dog's liver. It can be fatal for your Yorkie if not treated.

Yorkshire Terrier Food

Ensuring you feed your Yorkie with proper food, is vital in maintaining its health. You also need to know when and how much food to give. The amount of food and the type of activities your Yorkie partakes in, influences how much you need to feed it. Yorkies usually need two to three feedings daily. Avoid waiting too long between meals. It's not advisable to go for more than 6-8 hours between meals during waking hours. Underfeeding your Yorkie can lead to low blood sugar and stomach problems.

How Much to Feed a Yorkshire Terrier

There is no hard rule to only feed your Yorkie a certain portion based on its age, although a Yorkie puppy needs at least 45 to 55 calories per pound of body weight, per day. So, a 10-pound Yorkie needs approximately 500 calories, per day. A good rule of thumb to follow is to feed it ¼ to ½ cup of dog food, per feeding, but check your labels to calculate the calories. It is always best to check with your veterinarian if your Yorkie has any specific dietary needs, based on its health history.

Eukanuba Yorkshire Terrier

At the time of this writing, one of the better formulas is called Eukanuba Yorkshire Terrier. It is a brand of dog food created by Mars, Inc. specifically for Yorkshire Terriers. It addresses most of the Yorkies needs, which include dental and skin health, coat condition, and a well-nourished immune system. Eukanuba is packed with omega fatty acids, zinc, copper, antioxidants such as vitamin E, and FOS, a natural probiotic that strengthens protection in the digestive tract. It comes in kibble type, with chicken as the primary ingredient. It is recommended for adult Yorkies one year and older.

Next is a table of Eukanuba's ingredients and nutritional content. If you can't find this particular formulation or prefer another brand that is fine, just look for one with a similar nutritional profile.

Ingredients	Nutritional Content
Chicken, Chicken By-Product Meal, Corn Meal, Ground Whole Grain Sorghum, Brewers Rice, Chicken Fat (preserved with mixed Tocopherols, a source of Vitamin E), Dried Beet Pulp, Ground Whole Grain Barley, Chicken Flavor, Fish Meal, Dried Egg Product, Fish Oil (preserved with mixed Tocopherols, a source of Vitamin E), Potassium Chloride, Salt, Sodium Hexametaphosphate, Fructooligosaccharides, Dicalcium Phosphate, Flax Meal, Calcium Carbonate, Brewers Dried Yeast, Minerals (Ferrous Sulfate, Zinc Oxide, Manganese Sulfate, Copper Sulfate, Manganous Oxide, Potassium Iodide, Cobalt Carbonate), DL-Methionine, Choline Chloride, Vitamins (Ascorbic Acid, Vitamin A Acetate, Calcium Pantothenate, Biotin, Thiamine Mononitrate (source of vitamin B1), Vitamin B12 Supplement, Niacin, Riboflavin Supplement (source of vitamin B2), Inositol, Pyridoxine Hydrochloride (source of vitamin B6), Vitamin D3 Supplement, Folic Acid), Vitamin E Supplement, Beta-Carotene, Rosemary Extract	Crude Protein (min) 28.0% Crude Fat (min) 18.0% Crude Fiber (max) 4.0% Moisture (max) 10.0% Calcium (min) 1.05% Copper (min) 18 mg/kg Zinc (min) 215 mg/kg* Vitamin E (min) 140 IU/kg Beta Carotene (min) 10 mg/kg Omega-6 Fatty Acids (min) 1.75%* Omega-3 Fatty Acids (min) 0.27%*

Yorkshire Terrier Puppy Food – What Is the Best Type?

When your Yorkie is old enough (between four to five weeks old) to transition from liquid to solid food, you may start it with a base that is the same as what its mother has been eating. You may also add a quality dog milk replacement, though you should stay away from other animal milk, like goat or cow milk. After a few days, you may reduce the amount of milk, until your Yorkie can eat a solid food diet.

By the eighth week, your Yorkie can eat manufactured dog food, without altering its consistency. There are many varieties available in the market, and it can be confusing to choose the best one to give to your Yorkie.

Here some tips to help you in buying dog food for your Yorkie:

- **Watch out for chemical additives.** If you see artificial coloring, flavors, and preservatives listed in the ingredients, give this a pass and look for another dog food.
- **Be cautious about by-products.** Animal by-products can come from unused body parts such as hooves, intestines, and kidneys. Some are even from road kill or dead poultry that did not make it to manufacturing houses. They add these things to supplement the required protein levels in dog food products.
- **Beware of fillers.** These are used to make the food fuller but do not have any nutritional value. These are immediately converted to waste since the body does not absorb any nutrients. Too many fillers in a food formulation can even cause malnutrition.

Yorkie Veterinary Care – What does This Breed Need?

The veterinarian is your partner in keeping your Yorkie healthy. His or her clinic should be near your home and must be accessible to you, especially when your Yorkie has an accident or in an emergency. The veterinarian should give you a contact number in cases of emergency and if his or her clinic is closed.

You will need to make your first visit to the veterinarian as soon as you get your Yorkie, whether you bought it from a breeder, or adopted it from a rescue shelter. The next vet session is when your Yorkie puppy needs to have its first round of vaccination shots. You will also be visiting his or her clinic at least once a year for check-ups.

Be aware of any symptoms that include diarrhea, vomiting, labored breathing, and seizures. These may signal symptoms of potentially fatal health issues. If you observe these, bring your Yorkie to the vet immediately.

Yorkie Vitamins – What does Your Dog Need?

Some supplements can be given to your Yorkie to enhance its health, including:

- Omega-3 and Omega-6 fatty acids – these can protect the skin and stimulate hair growth.
- Vitamin A – prevents skin drying
- B vitamins – some of these include B3 and B5, that enhance the skin's moisture retention ability. These also encourage regeneration of new skin cells.

- Vitamin E – keeps skin in excellent condition and the coat shiny
- Brewer's yeast - also increases skin's moisture content
- Garlic supplements – helps in repelling fleas
- Zinc supplements – prevents the skin from turning pale
- Carotenoids – can be sourced from carrots, sweet potatoes, and various red, yellow, and orange fruits and vegetables. These can also aid in improving your Yorkie's coat.
- Glucosamine and chondroitin – help absorb calcium, and improve joint health

These supplements can be obtained from natural sources like vegetables, or synthetically digestible sources, like gel capsules. Always check with your veterinarian for the best and safest supplement to give to your Yorkie.

Vaccinations – What does Your Yorkie Need?

Vaccinations are vital to keeping your Yorkie protected from certain diseases, especially contagious ones. Vaccination should start during puppyhood, as this is when the immune system is still developing. Your veterinarian will help you determine the optimal schedule for your Yorkie.

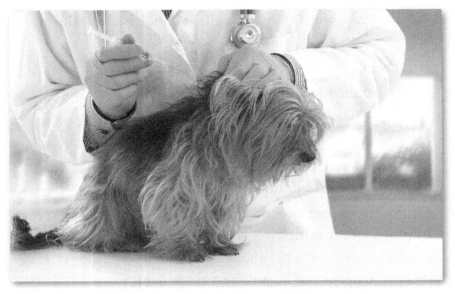

*Vaccinations are vital to keeping your Yorkie protected
from certain diseases, especially contagious ones.*

Here are some recommended vaccinations that your Yorkie
will benefit from, and the most common ages at which they are
administered:

- 6 to 7 weeks: distemper, measles, parainfluenza; optional:
  bordetella
- 10 to 12 weeks: DPHPP, adenovirus, parvovirus; optional:
  coronavirus, leptospirosis, Lyme disease
- 12 to 24 weeks: anti-rabies

How Can You Keep Your Yorkie Healthy?

Now that you have gained essential knowledge from this chapter
and the previous ones, you now have an understanding of
Yorkie essentials. To recap, always check with your veterinarian

throughout your Yorkie's life, and be quick to report any symptoms.

Proper care includes nutritious food and supplements, vaccinations, and knowing the warning signs of possible medical issues. You must also commit to providing routine physical activities such as exercise and games, to keep your Yorkie active. Grooming is also essential to keep your Yorkie health and to avoid skin irritation and dryness that may lead to infection. Keep your Yorkie's living space clean and safe from any hazardous items. Never give chocolate and other inappropriate snacks to a Yorkie, as these can cause poisoning.

CHAPTER 10
Training Yorkies – Obedience Training

Yorkshire Terriers can show stubbornness, by not listening to your commands and barking incessantly when undisciplined. Because of their adorable appearance, owners tend to spoil them and neglect to reprimand them, when they exhibit undesirable behavior. These attitudes may go on until adulthood, and if this happens, it may be too late to correct your Yorkie's undisciplined ways.

*Yorkshire Terriers have a reputation for being
hard to train. Ensure you start early!*

Therefore, training must be conducted while your Yorkie is in its puppyhood if possible, to ensure the best results. To succeed in training your Yorkie, you must be prepared with the equipment and items that allow for optimal training. Set a consistent schedule for training and commit to it. Patience will be an integral part of this process.

Yorkie Items for Training – What You Need to Have Before Starting Training

There is a set of items you need to obtain before starting to train your Yorkie. Having these things will ensure a smooth flow, as you will not have to stop in the middle of training. This will also make training more effective and efficient.

- **Treats.** These are given to your Yorkie when it has successfully performed a command. This serves as positive reinforcement and creates a pleasant association to the activity. The best types of dog treats are made with natural ingredients. You may even use fruits (review Chapter 6 – Yorkshire Terrier Snacks – What Can You Give Your Dog?). Make sure the treats you give are tiny portions that are easy and quick to chew and swallow. The small servings will also not make it feel full immediately.

- **Clicker.** This produces a snappy clicking sound. In obedience training, it can help direct your Yorkie to perform a desirable behavior. You can also complement the moment you give out a treat to the sound of a click. Your Yorkie will be able to remember the behavior you want when it hears the clicker.

Yorkie Behavioral Problems – What are the Things You Need to Address?

There are some behavioral issues that your Yorkie can display and can carry to adulthood. These can cause a rift or disturbance to the harmony of living with your Yorkie. Some of these attitudes can even be harmful and result in injury. These habits can be rectified through obedience training. It will demand patience, energy and time for your part to succeed in this. If you feel that you do not have enough time to devote to obedience training, or the skills needed to do so, seek a professional dog obedience trainer to help you properly train your Yorkie.

- **Excessive Barking.** Yorkies are known to be yappers – incessantly barking to call your attention, soothe themselves because of anxiety, a way to display their aggression or discomfort, reacting to loud noises or other stimuli that can surprise them, and display territorial control. If it is excessively growling, howling, and whining, it is best not to allow this behavior to continue unchallenged.

If your Yorkie is doing this, observe first what causes it to bark incessantly. Once you have identified it, remove or reduce the trigger. Should there be a need to punish your Yorkie to rectify this behavior say a clear and firm "no!" or "stop!" command and squirt water on the dog.

- **Destructive Chewing.** This can be caused by a variety of reasons. If your Yorkie is still a puppy, this is its way of relieving the pain when it is teething. Another reason is your Yorkie is bored and has to channel its pent-up energy. This manifests by your Yorkie chewing everything that comes into its path. You will need to set a clear boundary on the things that it can chew on, and what must not be touched at all. When you see your Yorkie attempting to gnaw at your items, command an assertive "no!" or "stop!" and remove the item from its mouth. Toss a toy near it as a distraction, and let it take the toy, instead of your item. You can also reduce this damaging trait by lowering your Yorkie's energy, via taking it out for exercise or walks. Also, do your part by keeping your possessions appropriately stored, where your Yorkie cannot access them.

- **Biting.** This can be your Yorkie's defense mechanism to stop whatever stimuli are distressing it. However, you will still need to discipline it to prevent from escalating to aggression. If you find you Yorkie biting you when you try to approach it, or when taking certain items that it has caught in its mouth, then you need to respond to the situation with a firm command and lightly tapping its neck.

- **Aggression.** This can manifest through biting, nipping, growling and barking. Yorkies tend to naturally display these habits because of their past duties as ratters. This can be especially harmful when your Yorkie shows aggressive behavior towards larger and fiercer dogs. The best way to prevent this is to socialize your Yorkie early on. If you can, reduce and eliminate triggers that cause your Yorkie to react in this manner. To control your Yorkie's aggression, it is important to assert your leadership through assertive commands and consistency, which will ingrain respect and obedience.

- **Leash pulling.** This happens when your Yorkie, clad with its harness and attached to the leash, suddenly sprints forward. The control should be in your hands, and when you allow your Yorkie to continue this behavior, you are transferring that power to your dog. An ideal scenario for a good leash habit is your Yorkie being able to walk by your side and stopping when you stop. Always let your Yorkie walk by your side, and reward it with a treat, when it does so.

Some of these behaviors that your Yorkie may exhibit are signs that something is distressing it, which could involve medical concerns. It could also be caused by past traumatic experiences, in which it remembers negative feelings when it is exposed to certain triggers. Always seek the advice of your veterinarian and professional dog trainer, to address these problems efficiently.

Training a Yorkie Puppy

Training a Yorkie in its puppyhood is the optimal period, to help it learn all the essential skills and commands required. Working with a puppy lets you start with a clean slate. This means you do not need to rectify behavioral problems that may have rooted in your dog for quite some time, and instead you can teach it to follow and obey you.

You can begin training your Yorkie puppy when it is two months old, starting with housebreaking training (review Chapter 8 – House Training Your Yorkie – What Skills does it Need to Know?). Once it has mastered this, you can move on to more advanced areas.

Here are some tips to make your Yorkie training more successful:

- **Create a fun and positive atmosphere.** Training will not be effective if you are stressed or tired. Conducting training sessions in these moods will make you impatient and make you prone to punishing your Yorkie, instead of praising or rewarding it. Your Yorkie will also be able to sense the same level of energy. Creating a positive experience will make your Yorkie more likely to look forward to the next training session.

- **Exercise before training starts.** Take your Yorkie out for a walk so it can release some of its energy, if it has been staying indoors for the whole day prior to training. This will enable your Yorkie puppy to focus more on the commands you are trying to teach it.

- **Consistency.** When you have established a routine for your training sessions, your Yorkie will grow accustomed to it, and this will help it understand what to expect. Consistency also applies with the commands you use.

- **Go easy with the treats.** When you give treats too often and too much, it can work against you. Too many treats can distract your Yorkie from performing the commands and instead cause it to get fixated on getting the treat.

- **Reward instead of rebuke.** Yorkies respond more to positive responses like treats and rewards than to being scolded. They will not understand the connection between their behavior and your yelling. Be patient with your Yorkie and celebrate milestones when they successfully master commands.

- **Assert your position.** It is important that you establish yourself as the leader of the "pack." You must exude calm and assertive energy, so your Yorkie will trust and obey you. You can do this by letting your dog perform commands that you have taught it before it can get its reward (meals, treats, toys, etc.).

Important Commands Your Yorkie Needs to Master

Certain commands are essential; below are some that it needs to master.

- **Heeling.** This behavior happens when your Yorkie walks calmly beside you. The dog must not decide which direction to take; that is your role, as the pack leader/owner. You are giving it control if you are allowing it to pull on the leash.

  To successfully teach it to heel, you need to be in front of the dog the moment the two of you step out of the door. Using a short leash can help you do this. Aside from edible items, a form of reward is letting your dog sniff around. When it has respected you as the leader and walks closely behind or beside you, give it some time to smell its surroundings. After the walk, you can give your Yorkie its meal as a reward for the "work" it has done.

- **Sit.** This command is vital when you need your dog to be calm and still. A scenario where is useful is when you set your Yorkie down, and you need to get some items from your car. This command will help prevent it from darting off anywhere.

To do this, grab a treat in your hand and hold it close to the dog's nose. Move your hand upwards and let your Yorkie follow your hand. This will cause its bottom to move lower. When it is in a sitting position, firmly command "sit!" so your Yorkie will associate that word with the action. Give it the treat and praise it if it has successfully performed the command.

- **Stay.** This command trains your dog to have self-control. Your Yorkie must have mastered the "sit" command before moving on to this. Order your dog to "sit," and with an open palm say "sit." Slowly take a few steps back and give it a reward if it stays in place. You may increase the distance between you and your Yorkie as it masters this command.

- **Come.** In case your Yorkie moves far away from you or loses grip on the leash, this command will make it come back to you. To do this, put the collar and leash on your dog. Lower yourself to its level and say "come," while lightly pulling on the leash. When it comes near you, reward it with a treat. Once it has mastered this with the leash, you can take it off, and practice the command in a safe and enclosed area.

- **Down.** This command makes your Yorkie take on a submissive position and relaxes it when it is fearful or anxious. This is important to help your Yorkie relax when you have guests in your house, and it reacts aggressively. Grasping a treat in your hand, make your dog sniff it first, and then move your hand slowly to the floor. Make sure your dog is following your movement and slide your hand along the floor to encourage its body to do the same. Once it is in the "down" position, reward it with the treat and show praise.

Yorkshire Terrier Training – What are the Best Strategies?

Training will be an investment on your part and that of your Yorkie. You will be spending some time, energy and money, so it is best to proceed as efficiently as you can. Below are some strategies you can apply during training, to make it easier and more effective.

- **Keep sessions brief.** This works for you and your Yorkie's benefit. 30 to 45 minutes for a basic obedience training session is too long. It will make you impatient, and your Yorkie bored. This could render the training ineffective. Instead, you can have short sessions of 5 to 10 minutes, spread throughout different times of the day.
- **Set realistic expectations.** Don't expect your Yorkie to perfect a command in one training session. Set mini-goals during each session, which can serve as small steps, until your Yorkie has finally mastered the command.
- **Set rules and stick to them.** Establish what behavior your Yorkie should and should not exhibit. You should set

guidelines for yourself when you allow yourself to hand out treats and give praise. Remember that overdoing these things can make your Yorkie distracted and confused as to which behaviors to exhibit.

- **End on a positive note.** This will make both you and your Yorkie look forward to the next training session. Even if your Yorkie did not completely get the lesson perfectly, end it with a command that it has already mastered, so you can still reward and praise your dog as you end the session.

CHAPTER 11

Yorkshire Terrier Breeding

This is part of your tasks of being a responsible Yorkshire Terrier owner to decide if you would like to breed. This decision will prompt you to take actions vital to your Yorkie health, and that of its future offspring.

If you are thinking of letting your Yorkie breed "at least once in its life" and "let it experience the whole reproductive process," then you have the wrong idea of breeding. A breeder's goal is to improve the genetic condition of the breed. This entails many hours of research, examination, and selection to eliminate the unfavorable conditions of the breed slowly. This is a serious matter and requires a lot of responsibility and resources from you.

What are Your Responsibilities as a Yorkshire Terrier Breeder?

Once you have obtained your Yorkie, decide if you will let it breed or not. If you are not interested in caring for a dam (mother dog) or sire (father dog) and are not concerned with the whole breeding process, you will need to spay/neuter your Yorkie.

Once you have obtained your Yorkie, decide if you will let it breed or not, considering the work and research required for the process.

Should you decide to let your Yorkie breed, first determine if it is optimally healthy to do so. You have to screen its health condition and history and ensure that it does not have any fatal hereditary medical concerns that can potentially be inherited by its offspring.

You will constantly be checking with your veterinarian at every stage of your dam's pregnancy. This will aid in securing your Yorkie's health, and that of her puppies. You will be able to respond to any possible health concerns and take action before things escalate.

You should never view breeding as your primary source of income. Puppy mills and pet shops typically have this perspective and execute unethical means to produce pups. Your love for the breed and the goal of improving its line should be your highest motivations for becoming a Yorkshire Terrier breeder.

Yorkshire Terrier Full Grown – When Can They Start to Breed?

From the sixth month to its second year after birth, your Yorkie is in its adolescent stage. If you did not spay/neuter your Yorkie, it would start to exhibit sexual behavior. The safest time to start breeding your Yorkie is when it has settled into adulthood, around two to three years old.

Yorkie Male – How to Take Care of One for Breeding

Male Yorkies grow into sexual maturity faster than females. As a safety precaution, do not let your male Yorkie start breeding until at least one year old.

Since male Yorkies develop sexually at a younger age, they might start pursuing female dogs in heat (regardless of the breed). You should be careful with your dog during this period, and not let him go near any female dogs that you do not intend to allow to be impregnated. He might even find ways to escape your home to track the scent of fertile female dogs, even if they are miles away. Keep your doors closed and set up boundaries to prevent him from leaving your home at this time.

Female Yorkie – How to Prepare Her for Breeding

A female Yorkie can have her first heat (the stage in the female's reproductive cycle where she becomes receptive to males), as early as four months from birth. This would be too early for her to engage in copulation and may cause serious complications to her and the pups, should she become pregnant. The ideal time for her to breed is when she is at least one year old and after her second heat.

When she gets older than five, it is best to retire her from breeding and let her rest. This should be considered on a case by case basis, however. If she was able to produce more than three litters from between the ages two to five years, then instead, she should not be permitted to breed when she becomes seven years old and beyond. If she has only produced one litter between her fourth and fifth year, she can still produce healthy pups when she reaches seven years old. This can be a different case for each Yorkie, so you should always check with your veterinarian.

When your female Yorkie has retired from breeding, it is recommended to spay her. This can help prevent ovarian and breast cancer.

Baby Yorkies – How to Take Care of New-Born Yorkie Puppies

Infancy is the most delicate and vulnerable stage of a dog's life. As a breeder, you need to prepare to give the required care at each stage of the pups' growth.

- **Birth to three weeks old.** Newborn pups should be gaining weight from the day of their birth and onwards. It is expected that they will gain around 0.07 to 0.70 oz. (2 to 20 gm.), during the first few days. Watch out if the pup does not gain weight or loses weight. Keep the dam's nutrition at its best by feeding her with quality dog food, and having fresh water near her, at all times.

- **3 to 4 weeks.** Allow the mother to take care of her pups with minimal intervention from you. Your role during this period is to supervise how things are going and keep them running smoothly. If you see a pup having lesser time than its littermates feeding because it is being pushed away, you can set the other littermate aside for a while and let the pup feed. There may be situations where the pups will be bottle-fed upon the advice of your veterinarian. Keep in mind that the pups must be able to get a constant supply of nutrition, or else it can lead to health concerns, such as hypoglycemia (sugar levels dropping at a rapid rate). Gently trim the pups' nails when they get too sharp to help prevent injury to the mother or the other puppies.

  It is also during this time that the pups' eyes start to open, and they will begin to crawl around. Provide them space where they can explore and exercise the muscles in their legs. Keep their whelping area clean, at all times.

*Pups that are four to five weeks old will become more
playful and may start to tumble and nip at each other.*

- **4 to 5 weeks.** The pups will begin to wean (gradually removing
  the pup at this point from being solely dependent on its
  mother's milk.) You can start to introduce formula milk and
  transition to solid food. The pups will become more playful at
  this point and may start to tumble and nip at each other. The
  mother will discipline her pups when play gets too rough. It
  is also best to let the pups get used to human touch, so they
  must be gently held daily. Other things that the pups will
  need to be accustomed to is being washed by a washcloth,
  being touched in its mouth and teeth (for dental care), and
  paws (for nail trimming). They should also grow comfortable
  with common household noises, so they won't feel anxious
  when they are exposed to these, in the future.

- **6 weeks.** The pups should ideally have a food portion
  consisting of an 80:20 ratio of solid food and milk.

Yorkshire Terrier Breeders – How to Find Reputable Ones?

The first place you may want to check is the Yorkshire Terrier Club of America. This organization has a list of member breeders who signed and agreed to comply with the Code of Ethics and Conduct for Breeding. Please take note that YTCA does not guarantee the health or services that these listed breeders provide and does not assume any liability concerning agreements between the aspiring Yorkshire Terrier owner and the YCTA members. It will be your responsibility as the buyer to take due diligence in securing the dog's health and temperament.

Another venue where you can find reputable breeders is by attending Yorkshire Terrier dog shows in your vicinity. Most reputable breeders are active in dog shows that involve conformation and obedience. You will see the best Yorkie appearance and temperament and observing these qualities can help you select a suitable puppy for yourself. You will also get the chance to connect with them and ask questions about breeding and finding other breeders. You can also inquire about the reputation of the breeders in the community.

When you have identified and located a Yorkie breeder, it is imperative that you visit the breeder's kennel and see the environment where his or her Yorkies live. You want to see a clean, well-supplied, and loving home.

The breeder should also be able to present you with AKC registration and documents. This will assure you that the dog in question, is purebred. The breeder must have these certifications before they allowed their dogs to breed, or else their puppies will be ineligible for registration.

You will need to discuss with him or her the medical history, condition, and temperament of their dogs and yours. Talk to them about how their dog and yours can complement each other in reducing medical conditions that are hereditary and minimize unfavorable temperament. They need to be knowledgeable about Yorkshire Terriers, and you can find this out by asking the right questions.

Below are some qualities that the breeder's dogs must show:

- The adult dogs and puppies must look like the breed they represent! Show-quality dogs will have better conformation, and you must be able to recognize that it is a Yorkshire Terrier immediately. Some breeders may be dishonest and won't disclose if the puppies are from a mixed-breed pair. Other litters are produced from a lineage of poor quality breeding, and therefore they hardly look like Yorkies anymore!

- They should at least have the coat colors that adhere to the AKC standard (see the breed standards section, chapter 2 for more information).

CHAPTER 12

Different Yorkie Mix Breeds

Over the years there has been an emergence of partial Yorkshire Terrier, hybrid dogs. Also known as "designer dogs," these pups are produced by breeding a purebred Yorkshire Terrier, and a purebred dog of a different breed. This chapter will discuss the popular Yorkshire Terrier designer dog mixes.

More than their adorable and unique appearance, designer dogs have a higher chance of being healthier, than purebred ones. A factor that can cause this is that the gene pool becomes more varied compared to the inbreeding that usually happens to purebred dogs.

Another variable to consider with partial Yorkies is that you will not be able to fully anticipate what their temperament and appearance will be. Many factors come into play that affects this, which include the other breed parent's genetic history, how this blends with the Yorkie, and which traits show up in the offspring.

Remember that not all breeds are conducive to mate with a Yorkie. An example is choosing dogs that are bigger in size. This can certainly lead to health concerns that can be fatal to your Yorkie and its pups.

The designer dogs described in this chapter are recognized by the DBR (Designer Breed Registry), IDCR (International Designer Breed Registry), DDKC (Designer Dogs Kennel Club) and ACHC (American Canine Hybrid Club).

Yorkie Shih Tzu

These dogs are known by different names – Shorkie Tsu, Shorkie, and Yorkie Tzu. These dogs are produced by breeding a purebred Yorkie and a Shi Tzu.

An adult Shorkie's height can measure up to 14.96 in. (38 cm.). They can also weigh between 2.20 to 17.63 lbs. (1 to 8 kgs.). Shorkies have similar lifespans with purebred Yorkies, which is 12 to 15 years. Coat colors can range from black, red, brown, golden white with black, and beige.

Grooming demands are the same as with purebred Yorkies. Since these two breeds have naturally long coats, they need to be combed and brushed regularly.

Yorkie Bichon

Yorkie Bichon dogs are born from a purebred Yorkshire Terrier and Bichon Frise.

An adult Yorkie Bichon can grow to a height of 9 to 12 in. (22.86 to 30.48 cm.), while weighing around 6 to 8 lbs. (2.72 to 3.62 kg.). They also have similar life expectancy with the

Yorkshire Terriers, which is approximately 10 to 12 years. Their temperament is known to be active, energetic, playful, curious, loving, and smart.

The Yorkie Bichon's coat is dense, full and soft. They do not cause too many allergies compared to other breeds. Unlike the Yorkie which sheds minimally, this hybrid is prone to shedding. Daily brushing is needed to maintain its coat.

Maltese Yorkie

Maltese Yorkies are produced from a purebred Yorkshire Terrier and a Maltese. Other names for this hybrid are Morkie, Yorktese, Yortese, Yorkiemalt, Malkie, and Maltiyork.

Maltese Yorkies can grow to a height of 5.90 to 9.84 in. (15 to 25 cm.) and weigh around 5.79 to 10.20 lbs. (2 to 4 kg.). Their lifespan is about 12 to 15 years. These dogs are loyal, loving and affectionate.

This designer dog has a straight, thin, long, and silky coat. Shades can be white, black, and brown with tan. As with the previous designer dogs, daily brushing is necessary, to maintain the quality of its coat.

Maltese Yorkies are susceptible to dental problems and thus need daily dental care, to avoid these. They can also be sensitive to digestion issues, skin issues, and issues with the kneecaps.

Yorkie Chihuahua

The Yorkie Chihuahua is bred from a purebred Yorkshire Terrier and a Chihuahua. Other names for this hybrid dog include Chorkie, Yorkiechi, Yorkie Chi, and Chiyorkie. The mix has started to appear since the early 1990s.

An adult Chorkie can grow to a height of 5.90 to 9.05 in. (15 to 23 cm.), and weigh between 6.61 to 13.22 lb. (3 to 6 kg.). The life expectancy of Chorkies is 10 to 15 years.

Most Chorkies look more like a Yorkshire Terrier but have inherited their large ears, round head, and eyes, from the Chihuahua. Their bodies are tiny but well-built. This is a fairly healthy designer dog. However, the two different breeds share similar health issues.

The Chorkie's coat can come in black, gray, white, reddish, tan, brown, and merle. The quality of the coat may vary, but most Chorkies have a long silky coat with very few curls. This hybrid does not shed too much and will need regular brushing to keep it neat and tangle-free. Hair inside the ears can grow long, so it is important to gently trim it when it gets too long. Failing to do this can irritate the ears and cause infections.

Chorkies may have inherited an amplified Napoleon complex from their parents. They may exhibit aggression towards other bigger dogs, despite their small size.

Yorkie Poodle (Or Yorkie-Poo)

The Yorkie Poodle is bred from a purebred Yorkshire Terrier, and a Poodle. Another name for this hybrid is Yorkiedoodle.

An adult Yorkie Poodle's height can measure between 5.90 to 13.77 in. (15 to 35 cm.) and weigh around 1.36 to 2.26 lb. (3 to 5 kg). The average lifespan of this designer dog is 15 years.

Coat colors can come in brown, black, gray, white, and black with gold spots. The coat can appear long and silky, which is inherited from its Yorkie parent, and in some cases will appear curly, which would be from the Poodle side. They are not heavy shedders and do not cause too many allergies. Care for its coat includes scheduled trimming every one to three months, and it must regularly be brushed, to avoid matting.

The Yorkie Poodle's temperament is energetic, playful, brave, and smart. They comfortably fit into the family, get along well with children and other pets, and will not have problems adjusting to apartment living.

CHAPTER 13

Other Yorkie Information You Need to Know

This section covers additional information that you need to know about the Yorkshire Terrier. It discusses topics such as what miniature and teacup Yorkies are. It also discusses the advantages of belonging to a Yorkie club and lovers group, entering your Yorkie in show competition, and fostering a stronger bond with your Yorkie.

Miniature Yorkies and Teacup Yorkies – What are They and What You Should Know About Them?

Miniature and teacup Yorkies are dogs of the breed that are smaller than average, or normal height and weight. An adult teacup Yorkie only weighs around 2 to 3 lbs. (0.90 to 1.36 kg.), whereas the average weight of a normal Yorkie is around 5 to 7 lbs. (2.27 to 3.17 kg.).

Often there will be a smaller Yorkie, compared to its brothers and sisters in a litter. If the offspring were bred from normal and healthy purebred Yorkies, and the small size of the dog naturally occurred, then this should not be a problem. The issue arises when irresponsible and profit-driven breeders deliberately breed the smallest dogs until they get the tiniest possible version of the breed. They then market this as "miniatures" and "teacups," and sell them at a higher price.

Teacup Yorkies have a plethora of health issues
and will require more care.

Teacup Yorkies have a plethora of health issues and will require more care. These dogs live significantly shorter lives than normal. The average lifespan of standard Yorkie is 12 to 15 years, while teacups only live for about 2.5 to 3 years on average.

One such case of a teacup Yorkie was "Tiny Pinocchio." He became famous and an instant celebrity when he grazed the show stages of Oprah Winfrey and the Today Show. People beheld Tiny Pinocchio's size as a novelty. They thought that his 1 lb. (0.45 kg.) and 4.5 in. (11.43 cm.) frame was utterly adorable. However, Tiny Pinocchio only lived for two years.

Producing teacup dogs has caused controversy in the canine ownership and breeding world, and most responsible dog owners do not approve of such conduct. The AKC and other reputable dog kennels and groups do not even recognize miniature and teacup dogs.

Be careful of breeders and sellers who primarily focus on marketing and selling miniature and teacup Yorkies. If you truly love the breed, you will know that this abnormal size is a huge disadvantage for them. As long as someone is interested in buying these dogs, breeders and sellers will continue producing them.

Yorkshire Terrier Clubs and Yorkie Lovers Groups – Why and How to Join One?

Yorkshire Terrier Clubs and Lover Groups are organizations where breeders, owners, and enthusiasts of the breed relate to each other and have created a body of standards and operations.

Yorkshire Terrier Clubs are more formal organizations with sets of rules and regulations. They are mostly AKC-affiliated, and often conduct dog shows and competitions. The primary objective of these clubs is to preserve and protect the Yorkshire Terrier breed. They also aim to educate people about Yorkies and promote the breeding of dogs that are true to breed standard appearance and to ensure good health and temperament.

The most important aspect of belonging to a Yorkie club or group is being in the presence of people who are genuinely passionate about the breed. Joining one will enable you to connect with other breeders, owners, and enthusiasts. It will give you the opportunity to ask questions and learn from their experiences. Veteran members of these clubs will gladly share their information with you.

Requirements for entering a Yorkie organization will vary. Joining some clubs will be as easy as completing a membership form and paying a membership fee. Others will require a referral from their member, to vouch for you.

Becoming a member is not all about how it can benefit you, but also how you can give back to the club. Some of the responsibilities of becoming a club member are helping organize events, attending meetings, and participating in discussions on how to help improve the organization and make it better for every member and dog.

Yorkie Show Dogs – What do You Need to Know?

This section will focus on conformation dog shows. This type of competition judges how closely your Yorkie represents the official standard physical appearance of the breed. Judging is done based on a numbered scale.

For your Yorkie to be able to join conformation events, it must be at least six months or older. This is the ideal age where your Yorkie will start to exhibit adult appearance, and closer to the standard for judging.

One of the essential factors that will be looked at is your Yorkie's coat. It must appear silky, long, and flowing. The show dog is the required type of grooming style that your Yorkie must sport for this event. Other qualities that will be judged are the dog's bite, paws, bone structure, and gait.

Other Dog Competitions where You can Enter Your Yorkshire Terrier

The following Yorkie competitions are more active and require training for both the handler and the dog.

- **Obedience.** Your Yorkie will be assessed by how perfectly it executes tasks and commands. Some of these activities include heeling, coming, staying, retrieving objects, and keeping still while a physical exam is being conducted. Your Yorkie must be AKC-registered and at least six months old, to join this contest.

- **Tracking.** Your Yorkie is evaluated on how it can follow a scent to find objects. Each stage gets increasingly tricky, where the dog must navigate a longer track, more directional changes, and the scent harder to identify. The best time to start training your Yorkie for this contest is at four months of age, and it will be able to compete when it is at least six months old officially.

- **Agility.** The winner of agility competitions goes to the Yorkie who can swiftly complete an obstacle course that involves jumps, tunnels, weave poles, and other hurdles. Your Yorkie must be registered to the AKC, and at least one year old before it can compete in agility trials.

- **Freestyle.** This is one of the newer competitions where entertainment is more valued. This involves creating a choreographed dance with your Yorkie and performing it before a set of judges and audience.

If you are a new Yorkie owner and are set to participate in official competitions, you may want to start out at dog show matches. These are events where the results will not be recorded in your Yorkie's official dog show history. This allows you and your Yorkie to practice and get used to the competition atmosphere, before entering official contests.

How to Build a Stronger Bond with Your Yorkshire Terrier

More than providing for your Yorkie's basic needs, the best part of having it as a companion is building a strong relationship with it. By establishing this type of bond, you will truly know how loyal a Yorkshire Terrier is.

Both you and your Yorkie will benefit if you understand each other's body language. You will become more sensitive to how your Yorkie feels and you will be able to give it the care and attention it needs. Your Yorkie can also acknowledge you as the pack leader and show you the proper respect and obedience.

Training will always be an integral component of your Yorkie's relationship with you. Not only is this a tool for shaping your Yorkie's discipline, but also helps form your bond with it as you spend time in training and understanding its limitations.

*The best way of strengthening the bond between you and your
Yorkie is by experiencing new things together.*

Lastly, the best way of strengthening the bond between you and
your Yorkie is by experiencing new things as a team. Bring your
dog to new places and let it experience fresh environments. This
will create memorable moments for you and your Yorkie that will
be cherished for a lifetime.

Conclusion

More than its adorable features, the Yorkshire Terrier is a fierce and loyal companion. It came from humble beginnings during the Industrial Revolution and was later elevated to celebrity status because if its natural beauty and affectionate temperament.

Your responsibility as an owner is to give it proper care and nutrition. Yorkies are fairly healthy dogs with minimal health concerns. They need moderate physical activity and need to be given enough entertainment and obedience training to avoid becoming destructive.

Yorkies, like other small toy breeds, have a longer lifespan compared to other dog breeds. You have a real opportunity to form a partnership that you will enjoy for many years. Refer back to this book to guide you through every stage of acquiring and caring for your Yorkie. Good luck and have a fantastic journey with this beautiful breed!

Yorkies, like other small toy breeds, have a longer lifespan, compared to other larger breeds. With this in mind, you will be spending a lot of happy years with your Yorkie when you shower it with your affection and care!

Your Yorkshire Terrier Resource List

This resource list will give you details on breeder and rescue shelter locations, and further information on the Yorkshire Terrier breed.

Yorkshire Terrier Breeders in the USA

1. Brooksview Yorkshire Terriers
    http://www.brookviewyorkies.com/,
    based in Hoover, Alabama

2. Starshine Yorkies
    http://www.starshineyorkies.com/aboutus.htm,
    based in Alabaster, Alabama

3. Lee Ann Carruthers
    http://www.jlyorkies.com/main.htm,
    based in Bullhead City, Arizona

4. Scruffy's Toys,
    http://www.scruffystoydogs.com/,
    based in Phelan, California

5. Dumont Yorkshire Terriers,
    http://www.showbreeders.org/~Dumont/main.html,
    based in Wallingford, Connecticut

6. Foxfire Yorkshire Terriers,
   http://jenksfoxfire.com/,
   based in Sharon, Connecticut

7. Shirebourne Yorkshire Terriers,
   http://www.shirebourne.com/

8. Trio Yorkies,
   http://trioyorkies.com/,
   based in Delray Beach, Florida

9. Royal Crown Yorkies,
   http://www.royalcrownyorkies.com,
   based in Marietta, Georgia

10. Amineh Yorkies,
    http://aminehyorkies.homestead.com

11. Wolpert Yorkshire Terriers,
    http://www.wolpertsyorkshireterriers.com/,
    based in Columbia, Maryland

12. Jeni-Lanes,
    http://jenilanes.com/

Yorkshire Terrier Breeders in Canada

1. Yorkhaven,
   http://yorkhaven.ca/,
   based in Standard, Alberta

2. Yorkshire Puddin' Pups,
   http://yorkshirepuddinpups.com/,
   based in Barnwell, Canada

3. Veeveeyorkies,
   http://veeveeyorkies.wixsite.com/home,
   Calgary, Alberta

4. Sailomade Yorkies,
   https://www.sailormadekennels.com/,
   Saint John, NB.

5. Day Juel Kennel,
   http://www.dayjuel.com/,
   Oshawa, Ontario

6. Nanway's Yorkshire Terriers,
   http://nanway-yorkies.yolasite.com/,
   Hamilton, Ontario

7. Shoalcreek Kennel,
   http://www3.sympatico.ca/shoalyorkies/,
   Orangeville, Ontario

8. Rigair Perm. Reg'd
   http://www.rigair.com/,
   based in Toronto, Ontario

9. Rustic Pride,
   http://home.ica.net/~yorkies,
   Caledon, Ontario

10. Depasquiet Yorkshire Terriers,
    http://www.depasquiet.ca/,
    based in Hemmingford, Quebec

11. Cryca Kennels,
    http://crycakennels.com/,
    based in Asquith, Saskatchewan

Yorkshire Terrier Rescue Shelter in the USA

1. Yorkshire Terrier National Rescue, Inc.
   http://www.yorkierescue.com/
2. Save A Yorkie,
   http://www.saveayorkierescue.org/
3. Yorkie Rescue of America,
   https://yorkierescueofamerica.org/
4. Yorkie 911 Rescue,
   http://www.yorkie911rescue.com/
5. Florida Rescue Yorkie,
   http://www.floridayorkierescue.com/
6. Yorkie Rescue Houston,
   www.yorkierescuehouston.org/
7. Little Yorkie Rescue,
   https://www.littleyorkierescue.org/
8. Wren Yorkie Rescue,
   www.wrenyorkierescue.org/
9. Bluebonnet Yorkshire Terrier Rescue,
   www.savetheyorkies.org
10. Yorkie Friends Rescue,
    www.yorkiefriendsrescue.com/

Yorkshire Terrier Rescue Shelter in Canada

1. Happy Tails Rescue,
   http://www.happytailsrescue.ca/

Yorkshire Terrier Rescue Shelter in the United Kingdom

1. Many Tears Animal Rescue,
    http://www.manytearsrescue.org/dogslookingforhomes.php,

2. Dog Trust,
    https://www.dogstrust.org.uk/rehoming/

3. Mayflower Sanctuary,
    http://mayflowersanctuary.co.uk/

4. Waggy Tails Rescue,
    http://www.waggytails.org.uk/dogs.aspx

Made in the USA
Columbia, SC
20 October 2020